CAVENDISH PRACT[illegible]

The Magistrates' Court

SECOND EDITION

JULIE O'MALLEY

SERIES EDITOR

CM BRAND, SOLICITOR

Cavendish Publishing Limited

First published by Longman Law, Tax and Finance

Second edition published in Great Britain 1996 by Cavendish Publishing Limited, The Glass House, Wharton Street, London WC1X 9PX

Telephone: 0171-278 8000 Facsimile: 0171-278 8080

O' Malley, Julie,
The Magistrates' Court – 2nd edn – (Practice Notes series)
1. Criminal Courts – England

I.Title
344.2'051

ISBN 1 85941 301 3

Printed and bound in Great Britain

Contents

1 Introduction **1**

1.1 The magistracy 1

1.2 The role of the court 2

1.2.1 Adult criminal court 2

1.2.2 The youth court 2

1.2.3 Licensing 2

1.2.4 Civil court 2

1.3 Representation in court 3

1.4 The court clerk 3

1.5 Jurisdiction 4

1.6 Open court and court reporting 4

1.7 Basic definitions 5

1.8 Abbreviations 8

2 Magistrates' court procedure – criminal **10**

2.1 Summary offences 11

2.1.1 Entering a plea 12

2.1.2 Guilty pleas 12

2.2 Summary trials 12

2.2.1 Prosecution case 12

2.2.2 Submission of no case to answer 13

2.2.3 Defence case 13

2.2.4 Ajudication 14

2.3 Offences triable either way 14

2.3.1 Advance information 14

2.3.2 Mode of trial determination 15

2.4 Transfer and committal procedures 17

2.4.1 Transfer procedure 17

2.4.2 Committal procedure 18

2.5 Indictable offences 20

2.6 Adjournment procedure 20

2.7 A timetable for proceedings in the magistrates' court 20
2.7.1 Adjourments 21
2.7.2 Custody 21
2.7.3 Summons 21
2.7.4 Service 21
2.7.5 Appeals 21
2.8 Evidence 22
2.8.1 Witnesses giving evidence 22
2.8.2 Written statements and admissions 23
2.8.3 Other admissible evidence 24
2.8.4 Exclusion of evidence 24

3 Sentencing 25
3.1 Powers 25
3.2 Procedure 25
3.3 Sentencing options – general 26
3.3.1 Imprisonment, suspended, concurrent or consecutive, part suspension 27
3.3.2 Deferred sentence 27
3.3.3 Community service order 28
3.3.4 Probation order 28
3.3.5 Fines 29
3.3.6 Discharge 30
3.3.7 Breach of orders 30
3.3.8 Other penalties 30
3.4 Sentencing of juveniles/persons under 21 31
3.4.1 Detention in a young offender institution 31
3.4.2 Attendance orders 32
3.4.3 Committal for sentence 32
3.4.4 Ancillary orders 33
3.5 Mental health provisions 34
3.5.1 Hospital order (Mental Health Act 1983) 34

4 Bail 37
4.1 Time limits 39
4.2 Checklist for answering bail objections 40

5 Advocacy practice **41**

5.1 Prosecuting 42

5.1.1 The CPS file 42

5.2 Prosecution checklist 43

5.3 Defending 44

5.4 Defence checklist 45

6 Alternative procedures **47**

6.1 Binding over 47

6.2 Contempt of court 48

7 Principle offences **50**

8 Costs and legal aid **55**

8.1 Costs 55

8.1.1 Costs against an opposing party 55

8.1.2 Defendant's costs from central funds 56

8.1.3 Prosecution costs from central funds 56

8.1.4 Costs against the defendant 57

8.2 Legal aid 57

8.2.1 Application for legal aid 58

8.2.2 Appeals 59

9 Appeals **60**

9.1 To the Crown Court 60

9.1.1 Procedure 60

9.2 To the High Court 61

9.2.1 Case stated 61

9.2.2 Judicial review 62

9.3 Criminal Appeal Act 1995 63

10 Road traffic offences **64**

10.1 Defendant not present 64

10.2 Sentencing, penalty points and disqualification 66

10.2.1 Endorsement 66

10.2.2 Disqualification 66

11 Problems in criminal proceedings **71**
11.1 Joint defendants/severance 71
11.2 Multiple offences, tying up – committing or remitting 71
11.3 Mode of trial 72
11.4 Guilty plea – disputed facts 72
11.5 Defendant failing to appear 72
11.6 Prosecutor failing to appear 73
11.7 Witness failing to appear 73
11.8 Amendments 74
11.9 Defendant unfit to plead 74
11.10 Equivocal pleas 74

12 Provisions for juveniles **75**
12.1 The youth court 75
12.2 Procedure 76
12.3 Adjournment, remand and bail 78
12.4 Sentencing 79
12.5 Juvenile checklist 79

13 Liquor licensing **80**
13.1 Procedure 81
13.2 Permitted licensing hours (LA 1964 Pt III including ss 59, 60, 62, 67A, 68, 70, 74, amended by LA 1988 s 1) 82
13.3 Persons not to be served 82
13.4 Refusal of licence, appeal, provisional licences 83
13.5 Types of licence 83
13.5.1 On licences 83
13.5.2 Off licences 84
13.5.3 Restaurant and residential licences 84
13.5.4 Residential licences 84
13.6 Transfer and removal of licences 85
13.7 Protection orders 85
13.8 Application to alter premises 86
13.9 Club licences, and other liquor licences 86

14 Betting and gaming licences **88**

14.1 Betting licences 88

14.1.1 Procedure 88

14.1.2 Bookmaker's permit 88

14.1.3 Betting office licence 89

14.2 Gaming licences 89

14.2.1 Notices required for gaming licence application 90

15 Matrimonial, domestic and child care proceedings **91**

15.1 The family proceedings court 91

15.2 Procedure 91

15.3 Costs 93

15.4 Examples of common applications 93

15.4.1 Maintenance 93

15.4.2 Orders relating to residence and contact with chidren 95

15.4.3 Personal protection orders and exclusion orders 95

15.4.4 Adoption proceedings 95

15.5 Child care proceedings 96

15.5.1 Procedure 96

16 Magistrates' courts in England and Wales **98**

17 Further reading **138**

1 Introduction

Proceedings in the magistrates' court come within criminal and civil jurisdictions. In this book the emphasis is primarily on criminal proceedings and only the principal categories of other proceedings are considered, with other volumes in this series looking more closely at road traffic offences and domestic proceedings. Practice and procedure are outlined in each part and the chapter on problems in criminal proceedings is intended to help where particular questions and difficult issues arise.

1.1 The magistracy

The magistrates' court is defined by the Magistrates' Courts Act 1980 s 148 as 'any justice or justices acting under any enactment, or by his or her commission under common law'. Justices are either lay persons appointed by the Lord Chancellor's office from the local community or stipendiary magistrates who are salaried professionals with a legal training.

The magistrates are triers of fact and law in the magistrates' court and therefore decide on all questions that arise. They have a duty to do so judicially and therefore any decision reached can be subject to judicial review as well as the subject of appeal to the Crown Court.

To hear a complaint or in order to try an information summarily the court must comprise at least two but no more than seven justices (MCA 1980 s 121). However, a single justice may discharge the functions of conducting a preliminary investigation or determining the mode of trial (MCA 1980 ss 4, 10 and 54). Where a stipendiary magistrate is appointed he has all the powers of two lay justices (Justice of the Peace Act 1979 s 16), except in licensing matters.

In criminal cases a lay bench will ordinarily comprise three justices whereas a stipendiary magistrate will sit alone. In other matters the size of the bench may be limited by statute and there are limits and rules imposed eg by the Juvenile Courts (Juvenile Court [Constitution] Rules 1954) which are considered in Section B. Limits also apply in certain Civil Proceedings, eg MCA 1980 s 66 states that a domestic proceedings court should not exceed three justices. Rules for composition of the bench in licensing cases are given in Chapters 13 and 14. In areas of the North West this function is the responsibility of the Chancellor of the Duchy of Lancaster (MCA 1980 ss 1–13).

1.2 The role of the court

1.2.1 Adult criminal court

Virtually all criminal proceedings pass through the magistrates' court at some stage. The role of the court will depend on the particular proceedings but the magistrates can be described either as examining justices for cases being committed to the Crown Court or as determining justices in cases tried summarily. The aim of the first section of this book is primarily to show how they perform these functions and to outline the function and practice of the legal practitioners appearing in front of them. Road traffic cases are considered but not in detail as these are also the subject of a separate volume in this series (see Hannibal and Hardy, *Road Traffic Law*, 2nd edn, Cavendish, 1996).

1.2.2 The youth court

The youth court, its composition, its role as a criminal court for juveniles and rules is covered in Chapter 12 of this book. The function of the court is the same as that in adult criminal cases.

1.2.3 Licensing

Magistrates sit in the licensing committee, or in court, to consider matters relating to liquor, betting and gaming licences described in Chapter 13, where their function is to evaluate on behalf of the local populace the validity of applications before them.

1.2.4 Civil court

Magistrates also sit to determine various matters of civil law, some of which are the subject of Chapter 15 of this book. Their role in such proceedings is to evaluate the evidence before them and to decide an appropriate remedy, assessing any conflict in evidence and taking into account the needs of any children involved.

1.3 Representation in court

In criminal proceedings the prosecution will usually be brought by the police through the Crown Prosecution Service created by the POA 1985. A private individual can initiate proceedings and he, his solicitor or his barrister may then appear. For the Crown Prosecution Service the representative will be a lawyer from their staff or a solicitor or barrister acting as an agent. For some offences the prosecution is brought by a government agency other than the Crown Prosecution Service, eg Customs and Excise, Inland Revenue, Local Authorities, etc.

Defendants may represent themselves in any case or be represented by any barrister or solicitor. At court the Duty Solicitor may be available to provide advice to an unrepresented defendant in matters which carry a custodial sentence (and may provide assistance on other matters if circumstances allow).

1.4 The court clerk

The clerk to the court is an official of the court with a legal training who is present in court principally to assist the magistrates in conducting the proceedings (JPA 1979 ss 25–30). In the minefield of court procedure his role in guiding the footsteps of others when matters of law arise can not be underestimated. However, he should not appear to the public to exert any undue interference over the bench. He should not, for example, retire with them when they consider their verdict, unless invited expressly and in open court to do so, especially where there is no point of law arising at this stage: Practice Direction [1953] 1 WLR 1416 and *R v Eccles JJ ex p Fitz Patrick* (1989) 89 Cr App R 324: *R v Birmingham Magistrates' Court ex p Ahmed* [1995] Crim LR 503, QBD (where convictions for receiving stolen goods and deception were quashed by an order for *certiorari* after breach of these rules).

The clerk's full duties are not defined by statute, but in practice he is often essential to the administration of justice. Some of the instant duties as to advising on points of law, procedure and practice arising are described by JPA 1979 s 28 and other duties in the Practice Direction [1981] 2 All ER 831. He will advise on points of law bringing to the attention of the court any point that may arise, and is expected to assist the unrepresented defendant but may not conduct his case. For example, if an unrepresented defendant makes an attack on the character of a prosecution witness the prosecutor, who alone is aware of any previous convictions of the defendant, should ask for an adjournment and, when the justices retire, the clerk and the prosecutor should explain the position to the defendant ie that he stands to put his own character and previous convictions in issue (CEA 1898 s 1(f)(ii)).

His duties do not by statute include taking notes in criminal proceedings but in *Lancashire CC v Clarke* (1984) Watkins LJ observed that he thought it incumbent on them to do so even though the parties have no right to inspect these notes. However, in certain circumstances, eg an appeal or a part heard case, such notes obviously greatly assist and can be read on request. It is imperative for him to make notes in domestic proceedings.

1.5 Jurisdiction

For indictable offences the territorial jurisdiction extends to the whole of England and Wales. For summary offences the jurisdiction of the court is local and limited to the county or London Commission Area that it serves (or the City of London) including any area within 500 yards of the boundary of that area. However, the court will have jurisdiction where the alleged offender is charged jointly with another who comes within the jurisdiction or the person is being dealt with for another offence within the jurisdiction.

Questions of exclusive jurisdiction and ouster of jurisdiction may also arise. In such cases once justices are acting in a case then any purported taking of jurisdiction by any other justice is void and a decision of one court renders the matter *res judicata* in another.

Civil jurisdiction is limited territorially in the same way as jurisdiction for summary offences. Where concurrent proceedings are in progress, for example in a county court, the magistrates' court should adjourn its proceedings until those proceedings have ended.

1.6 Open court and court reporting

Criminal proceedings are generally in open court and the public can only be excluded if it is in the interests of justice (MCA 1980 s 4, *Scott v Scott* [1913] AC 417). If an alleged indecent film is to be shown then the public can be excluded but there is no power to exclude the press in these circumstances (see Stones Justices Manual). There is, however, only limited access of the public to youth or family proceedings courts (CYPA 1933 ss 37, 47 and MCA 1980 s 69).

Reporting of proceedings is limited in a similar way, with criminal proceedings being reported freely except in limited circumstances. In the case of juveniles the name or details which may identify the offender cannot be published. In committal proceedings only certain prescribed formalities can be reported unless the court makes an order removing the restrictions. Such an order may be made on application by the defendant only if it is in the interests of justice to do so.

Reporting restrictions exist on sexual offences and offences against children where the anonymity of the victim is paramount. There are also restrictions on domestic proceedings, and contempt proceedings, and it is a contempt of court to breach these restrictions as well as to have in court any tape recording equipment, etc as outlined in Chapter 5.

1.7 Basic definitions

Adjournment	Suspension of the consideration of a case until some specified date, or a date unknown, when the case should be ready to proceed.
Advance information	Advance information of the prosecution case is information about the case against the defendant and it is his right to such information in cases which are triable either way. This may be by way of witness statements, or a summary of the evidence. The prosecutor may withhold information if he believes it would be abused by the defendant.
Alibi warning	A warning given to the defendant to inform him that should he intend at trial to forward an alibi as a defence to a charge, he should give notice of that alibi within seven days: CJA 1967 s11.
Charge	The formal accusation of an alleged offender with an offence, which accusation on a charge sheet forms an information. After being charged, the defendant may be held in custody or remanded on bail to his first court appearance.
Child	A person under the age of 14.

Committal	The hearing of a matter in the magistrates' court to examine a case as to whether or not there is a *prima facie* case to be heard in the Crown Court. This issue may be agreed by the defence in which case the committal is by s 6(2) CJA 1982 (a 'paper committal') rather than s 6(1) where evidence is heard. Prior to committal, the Crown Prosecution Service have a duty to prepare a number of copies of the evidence in the case, these being for the Crown Court, the Crown Court judge, and original copies for the magistrates. Extra copies are also prepared for the defendant and the prosecution, the whole comprising the committal papers or committal bundle. Proceedings for committal will be replaced by mode of trial and transfer proceedings (qv) which will be implemented in 1996.
DVLC printout	In matters involving motoring, the defendant is often required to produce his driving licence in court but fails to do so. In such cases the magistrates can only proceed to endorse the licence if there is present in court a certified printout from DVLC Swansea obtained by the police. If the printout is not available, it should be remembered that it is often only required because of this failure on the behalf of the defendant. Printouts take some time to obtain and this should be borne in mind when an adjournment is sought.
Either way offence	An offence which can be tried in the magistrates' court or the Crown Court. This issue is settled in a mode of trial determination.
Indictable offence	An offence which can be tried in the Crown Court. This includes either way offences and offences which are only triable on indictment (ie only triable in the Crown Court). If an indictable offence is to be tried in the Crown Court, the issue of whether there is a case to answer is first heard at the committal in the magistrates' court. Whether an offence is indictable, either way, or summary (see below) will depend upon its classification under the MCA 1980 Sched 1.

Information	Material laid before the court to initiate proceedings. It need not be in writing or on oath but it must specify or describe the offence without duplicity or uncertainty as well as the name and address of the party charged and the person laying the information. If the exact date or place cannot be specified then a period of time between stated days may be given and the place of commission omitted.
Juvenile	Anyone under the age of 17.
Juvenile bureau	A liaison committee comprising police officers and others which notifies a local authority of the report of a juvenile of an offence and collates reports then prepared by social services and educational welfare departments as well as results of police inquiries. They then make recommendations as to prosecution to a senior police officer who is responsible for the final decision.
Mode of trial proceedings	Proceedings to determine whether a case should be heard in the magistrates court or transferred to the Crown Court. These are regulated by the Magistrates' Courts Act 1980 ss 19–21 amended by the CJA 1991 and subject to National Mode of Trial Guidelines, the most recent version of which were issued in 1995.
Qualifying factors	Aspects of an offence which suggest that an offence should be heard in the Crown Court rather than the magistrates' court.
Recognisance	An obligation or bond acknowledged before some court of record, the object of which is to secure the performance of some act such as to answer to bail, to keep the peace, or be of good behaviour.
Summary offence	An offence which can only be tried in the magistrates' court. All summary offences have been created by statute eg common assault and not paying the television licence. Some summary offences may be tried on indictment (and *not* therefore in the magistrates' court) if CJA 1988 s 40 applies, and by s 41 if a defendant is pleading guilty to a summary offence that offence may be committed along with an indictable offence for trial at the Crown Court.

Summons	An order made by the court requiring the appearance of a person before it. That person may be the defendant or a witness. Summons are often issued at the beginning of an offence following the laying of an information and, in other circumstances, where a person fails to appear as described in Chapter 10. They are often used for road traffic cases as described in Chapter 10.
Surety	A sum pledged, usually by deed, by a suretor to satisfy the obligation of another person. If the latter fails to satisfy his obligation then all or part of the sum may be ordered forfeited by the court.
Transfer proceedings	Proceedings designed by CJPOA 1994 to transfer a case from the magistrates' court to the Crown Court which are yet to be implemented. Provision was to be made for written or, in particular circumstances, oral representations to apply for the case to be dismissed.
Warrant	An authority for the arrest of a person, or for their production at court as a witness or defendant. Magistrates' powers to grant warrants are described in Chapter 10 in the section on failing to appear.
Young person	A person who has attained 14 years and is under 17 years.

1.8 Abbreviations

APA	Affiliation Proceedings Act
BA	Bail Act
B(A)A	Bail (Amendment) Act
CA	Children Act
CAA	Criminal Attempts Act
CEA	Criminal Evidence Act
CJA	Criminal Justice Act(s)
CJPOA	Criminal Justice and Public Order Act
CLA	Criminal Law Act
CYPA	Children and Young Persons Act
DPMCA	Domestic Proceedings and Magistrates' Court Act
GMA	Guardianship of Minors Act
JPA	Justices of the Peace Act
LAA	Legal Aid Act

MCA	Magistrates' Courts Act
MHA	Mental Health Act
OAPA	Offences Against the Person Act
PA	Police Act
PACEA	Police and Criminal Evidence Act
PCCA	Powers of Criminal Courts Act
POA	Prosecution of Offences Act
TA	Theft Act

2 Magistrates' court procedure – criminal

Once charged the defendant, if released from custody, is bailed to the date of his first court appearance. If detained he must be brought before the magistrates' court as soon as is practicable and in any event no later than the first available court sitting, which will be the same or the next day (excluding Sundays, Christmas Day and Good Friday).

Other than a charge the defendant may have been brought to court on a summons or warrant following the laying of an information. In this chapter the procedure relating to charges is considered. For the procedure following a summons refer to Chapter 10 on road traffic offences as the procedure for criminal matters is the same.

At the first court appearance by the defendant the procedure followed will depend upon the nature of the charge. There are three categories of offence namely:

- Summary only offences ie those which can be tried only in a magistrates' court.
- Offences triable 'either way' ie those which can be tried either in the magistrates' court or in the crown court.
- Indictable only offences, ie those which can be tried only in the Crown Court.

In general these categories reflect the seriousness of the offences as can be seen by reference to the examples in Table 1 and the table of offences in Chapter 7.

Table 1 Example categories of offence

Summary only offences	*Offences triable either way*	*Indictable only offences*
Assault on a police constable PA 1964 s 51	Assault contrary to s 47 OAPA 1861	Grievous bodily harm with intent OAPA 1861 s 18
Driving without due care or attention	Reckless driving Driving while disqualified	Causing death by dangerous driving
Criminal damage under £5,000	Criminal damage over £5,000	Destroying or damaging property with intent to endanger life
Fare evasion	Theft	Robbery

Procedure differs according to the category of offence and therefore each will be dealt with individually. It is therefore helpful if practitioners know whether offences are summary only, either way or indictable only and the sentencing limits for the offence which information can be found in Chapter 7. The prosecutor should also be aware of the state of preparation of the case and have ready access to the information in the prosecution file when it is required by the court.

2.1 Summary offences

On the first appearance the matter may be adjourned at the request of the prosecution or defendant subject to the magistrates' discretion. The prosecution occasionally seek an adjournment at this stage, for example, so that police enquiries can be concluded, for scientific evidence to be obtained, for the case to be reviewed by the CPS legal staff or for sundry other reasons.

The defendant may seek and be granted an adjournment if, for example, he wishes to seek legal advice but unless there are exceptional circumstances such a request is likely to be refused, because if he pleads not guilty the case is almost invariably adjourned for trial. There is no right to advance disclosure for 'summary only' offences but in some cases it may be appropriate for the defendant to know something of the case against him, and in such an event disclosure is entirely at the discretion of the prosecutor.

2.1.1 Entering a plea

The majority of these offences proceed to the stage that a plea is entered by the defendant at his first appearance. The clerk of the court will read out the charge and the defendant is asked whether he understands and whether he pleads guilty or not guilty. Alternatively, a plea is entered at the first date when prosecution and defence are ready to proceed. For discussion of fitness to plead and equivocal pleas see Chapter 11.

2.1.2 Guilty pleas

If the plea entered is one of guilty the procedure for sentencing described in the next chapter is followed. In the course of the proceedings the court must satisfy itself that the defendant's plea is not equivocal. In certain instances, particularly if he is unrepresented, the defendant may in mitigation or otherwise disclose a defence to the charge. In such cases application should be made to the court to change the plea. Changes of plea in general are considered in Chapter 11.

Occasionally the facts of the case may be disputed, even though there is a guilty plea and it is then the function of the magistrates to hear the evidence and determine the version of events on which it will sentence (see para 11.4).

2.2 Summary trials

If the plea entered is one of not guilty then a date will be fixed for the trial. On the trial date the prosecution and defence will be expected to be ready to proceed on the charges previously put and have available all such witnesses as they require since magistrates are unlikely to grant any further adjournment unless there are exceptional grounds. If further charges are preferred on the day of the hearing then the defendant may be granted, on request, an adjournment to prepare his defence to that charge (Stones Justices Manual 1.33). The summary trial procedure is then entered into.

2.2.1 Prosecution case

The prosecutor opens the proceedings by giving a summary of the alleged offence, and then proceeds to call the first witness, then other witnesses and then any other admissible evidence.

In the trial the general burden of proving the case is on the prosecution. They must adduce evidence to prove each element of the offence and sufficient evidence so the bench is satisfied beyond reasonable doubt of the guilt of the defendant. Exceptions to this rule arise from certain statutes where the burden may shift. For example, if a defendant is charged with possession of an offensive weapon contrary to the Prevention of Crime Act 1953 s 1 the prosecution need only prove possession of an offensive weapon. The burden of proof then shifts to the defendant to show, on the balance of probabilities, that he had a lawful reason for the possession thereof. Another example arises where a defendant is charged with driving without insurance, where the prosecution need to prove beyond reasonable doubt only that the defendant was driving. The burden of proof then shifts to the defendant to prove that he was insured (Road Traffic Act 1972 s 142). Should he produce a document of insurance the burden shifts once more to the prosecution. Byelaws and statutory instruments are required to be proved by the production of an appropriate document, eg the HMSO publication or a 'gazette' (Documentary Evidence Act 1882 s 2).

2.2.2 Submission of no case to answer

After the prosecution case the defence may make a submission that the prosecution has failed to show that there is a case to answer, for example, that an element of the offence has not been proved, or that the evidence has been so discredited or is so manifestly unreliable that no reasonable tribunal could safely convict on it (Practice Note [1962] 1 All ER 448).

Typically, such a submission is made where evidence of identification has been adduced but may be described as unsatisfactory, or in assault cases where the roles of the protagonists has become unclear. The practice is, of course, not confined to these cases and experience alone is probably the best guide as to usage. The prosecution has the right of reply to the submission to present their argument to show that a *prime facie* case has been made out.

2.2.3 Defence case

After the prosecution case and submission of no case to answer, if any, the defence case is called. The defence advocate may make an opening speech, but will usually not do so, as it may lead to forfeiture of his closing speech (MCR 1981 r 13). The defence advocate will then proceed to call all such witnesses as he wishes. The defendant is called as any other witness but before any other witness for the defence. After all witnesses, any other admissible evidence is adduced, and the prosecution adduce evidence in rebuttal.

At the end of the defence case the defence advocate makes his closing speech commenting on the evidence and highlighting his client's case accordingly. If any point of law arises then the prosecutor may be allowed to comment and make any counter argument before the magistrates retire to consider their verdict.

2.2.4 Adjudication

At any point where magistrates are asked to adjudicate on a matter the decision is reached by majority verdict. For this reason an uneven number should sit wherever possible. If three justices are sitting then they are under a duty to come to a decision and if they fail to do so *mandamus* will lie.

Judicial knowledge or notice is allowed to be taken of any matter provided that it does not constitute evidence and magistrates can use such knowledge and any specialist knowledge they may have to enable them to interpret the evidence before them as well as to ask questions. In matters of law, or mixed fact and law, they may ask the clerk to assist by advising on the law. However, on questions of fact the decision should be reached from their own opinion alone, and it is for them to weigh the evidence and assess witnesses.

If they can not reach a majority decision (commonly if there are only two magistrates) then the case must be adjourned for rehearing before a reconstituted court, and there is no casting vote of a chairman or stipendiary magistrate.

2.3 Offences triable either way

As for summary offences the matter may be adjourned at the first appearance for further enquiries or for the defendant to seek legal advice. The defendant is also entitled to ask for advance disclosure of the prosecution case and an adjournment may be necessary to allow the preparation thereof.

2.3.1 Advance information

Following POA 1985, a defendant has the right to know in advance details of the evidence against him where the alleged offence is triable either way, and the procedure for this is laid out in the Magistrates' Courts (Advance Information) Rules 1985 (SI 1985/601). In the first instance the prosecution is obliged to provide the defendant with a written notice as to his rights to request advance disclosure. The notice informs him of this right and of the procedure for making a request.

The defendant may waive this right but where a request is made a requirement is imposed on the prosecution to furnish information by supplying a copy of the relevant parts of the witness statements or a summary of the relevant facts. The prosecution may withhold disclosure of any matter or fact if he considers that such disclosure would be abused by the defendant, eg intimidation of witnesses, etc.

Waiver of advance disclosure is appropriate where expedition of the matter is desired. Examples of occasions where waiver could be used are:

- If the intended plea is guilty, and the matter can then be dealt with on the day.
- If the defendant is electing Crown Court trial when a further delay prior to committal whilst the information is prepared and considered is not necessary or desirable, eg if the defendant is in custody.

Waiver is inappropriate if time to consider the case and take full instructions is necessary, eg in many cases where the defendant intends to plead not guilty, and if the defendant is unsure as to whether he wishes to elect trial in the Crown Court or magistrates' court.

Once advance disclosure has been served or waived the case proceeds to a determination of the mode of trial.

2.3.2 Mode of trial determination

Mode of trial determination is regulated by MCA 1980 ss 19–21. In making a mode of trial determination, the court will have regard to the nature of the case and whether the circumstances of the case make this a serious offence, or one which they would not have sufficient powers of sentencing, or whether there are other circumstances which suggest that a particular court would be the preferred venue. The prosecution should, therefore, make a submission as to whether the matter is suitable for summary trial, outlining salient features of the alleged offence such as the value of the goods involved or the extent of injuries, or the use of weapons. Particular reference should be made to 'qualifying factors (qv)' which indicate that trial at the Crown Court is more appropriate. The defence is then invited to make representations. In reaching their decision at this point, there are guidelines issued by the Lord Chief Justice which the magistrates should follow. The most recent version of these guidelines dates from 1955. However, the guidelines remain 'guidelines' only and do not infringe on the magistrates' duty to consider each case individually and on its own particular facts.

Principally, the guidelines are:

- that the matter should not be decided on the basis of convenience;
- where there is a conflict of evidence the prosecution version should be preferred;
- by CJA 1991 s 39(1) previous offences are relevant, possibly making it more unsuitable for summary trial;
- by CJA 1991 s 28 personal circumstances are relevant, possibly making it more suitable for summary trial. Offences to be taken into consideration are irrelevant, but if the counts are specimen charges this is relevant;
- complicated issues of fact or law will make the case more suitable for the Crown Court. Where two or more defendants are jointly charged each has an individual right to elect his mode of trial: *Brentwood JJ ex p Nicholls* [1992] 1 AC 1. However, where one or more defendants elects Crown Court trial this may result in the magistrates sending all for trial, although the *Nicholls* case emphasises that this is *not* an overriding consideration and this was confirmed in *R v Ipswich JJ ex p Callaghan* (1995), *The Times*, 3 April, QBD.

If the magistrates decide that the case should be heard in the Crown Court, then the case will be adjourned for transfer proceedings (or committal). If the magistrates feel able to deal with the case, then the defendant must still be warned that he can be committed for sentence if that is thought necessary. The defendant can then opt for trial in the magistrates court or the Crown Court. If he elects for the former then the matter proceeds as outlined for summary only offences. Where there are co-defendants, election by one of the two for Crown Court trial will mean that the other will be obliged to proceed to the Crown Court unless there are good reasons for severing the two. (Problems in determining mode of trial and changes of election are considered in Chapter 11.) If a jury trial is preferred the transfer procedure is followed.

If the case is to proceed to the Crown Court, then the prosecution will generally ask for an adjournment so that papers can be prepared. Prior to the return date, the defence will indicate whether they wish to apply for dismissal of the charges.

2.4 Transfer and committal procedures

Transfer proceedings were supposed to be replacing all committal proceedings in an attempt to simplify the court procedure.

2.4.1 Transfer procedure

The procedure to replace all committals by transfer for trial, pursuant to the CJPOA 1994 s 44, if ultimately introduced, will work as follows (although amendments have not made to the existing Magistrates' Courts Rules to cater for the proposed changes).

Essentially, if the case is an indictable offence or an either way offence to be heard in the Crown Court, then any initial appearance would be adjourned for the prosecution to prepare the transfer notice. The prosecution would serve a notice on the defendant and the court setting out the charges to be transferred. Attached to this are copies of the evidence and other relevant details. The defendant would then have the opportunity to serve an application for dismissal, which would be served on the prosecution, the court and any co-accused. The court would consider this application and written submissions accompanying it along with written submissions from the prosecution and the co-accused, if any. Oral representations would be accepted where the defendant is unrepresented and he would have to make his intention to make such representations clear in his application. Oral representations would also be considered if the defendant was represented and there were complexities or difficulties which appeared to require oral representations. The represented defendant would be expected to make an application for oral representation, which might be opposed by written submissions from the prosecution. In the event of oral representations from the defendant, the prosecution would be permitted to make oral representations in response.

Consideration of the transfer application would be followed by an adjudication. Where the magistrates find that there is insufficient evidence to put before a jury, the case would be dismissed. However, the court would have the power to amend the charges for trial if the evidence disclosed an offence other than that charged, whether the original charges were dismissed or otherwise.

2.4.2 Committal procedure

Currently, committal procedure continues as previously, except in those limited cases (complex fraud cases and those involving child witnesses) where transfers are already used instead of committal proceedings: CJA 1987 s 4 and CJA 1991 s 53.

If the case is one where committal proceedings are to be heard, these can be heard in the absence of the defendant provided that he is represented but he can not be committed in his absence, ie the order committing the matter to the Crown Court may not be made in the absence of the defendant (MCA 1980 s 4). Such a step will usually only be taken when the defendant is unable to attend through ill health or his behaviour is so unruly that he is ordered from the court. Provided that the committal is by way of MCA 1980 s 6(2) and that the defence have been served with committal papers seven days before the hearing, the defendant can be committed in the absence of any legal representative.

In MCA 1980 s 6(1) committals, the prosecution open the case by giving a brief outline of the facts and the evidence. The prosecution then call such witnesses as they need to prove a *prima facie* case although, with prior agreement from the defence, the evidence of some or all of the witnesses will be read out from witness statements. The witnesses called are in principle examined and cross examined in the same way as if in a trial and the prosecution should bear in mind that the defence may give evidence or call a witness and may be allowed to change his election (see Chapter 11). However, in practice a degree of flexibility exists and certain procedures are allowed to save time provided that the defendant fully agrees. Witnesses may simply be asked to prove their statements and then be cross examined on it, ie they take the oath and are shown their original statement and asked to verify the circumstances in which it was made, then they or the prosecutor read the statement to the court before being questioned by the defence. Additionally, certain agreed statements may be summarised for reading rather than simply read.

The evidence of such witnesses as are called is recorded precisely by the clerk and prepared as a deposition which must be signed and agreed by the witness before that witness is released. As each witness' evidence is concluded the prosecution and defence indicate whether they wish the witness to be fully or conditionally bound to appear in the Crown Court. It should be borne in mind that even though the evidence of some witnesses such as experts (analysts or doctors) may be uncontested it may be preferable for such witnesses to be fully bound.

Having heard the evidence the defence may make a submission that the prosecution have failed to make out a *prima facie* case against the defendant, ie that no jury properly directed could convict or could safely convict (*R v Galbraith* (1981) 73 Cr App R 124). Alternatively, they may call their own evidence and then make a submission, or if the matter is triable either way the defendant, if he wishes, may change his election and be tried in the magistrates' court (subject to the discretion of the magistrates).

After hearing the evidence the magistrates may then either commit the case to the Crown Court or discharge it as they decide. If the case is committed, the procedure follows that for MCA 1980 s 6(2) committals in that the alibi warning is given, bail is determined, etc. The court chosen will then depend on the issues, the seriousness of the case and the scheduling at the various courts (CJA 1981 s 75). Discharge of a case allows for the prosecution to be brought again if there is new evidence, but if the defendant applied to change his election and was allowed to do so the case may be dismissed and cannot be brought afresh.

MCA 1980 s 6(2) committals are used where the defendant concedes a *prima facie* case and require that:

- the charge be in written form and be read to the defendant at the hearing;
- all the evidence consist of written statements, with or without exhibits, conforming to conditions in MCA 1980 s 102 and copies be given to the defendant;
- each defendant be represented by a solicitor or barrister;
- there be no objection by or on behalf of the defendant to any prosecution statement tendered in evidence;
- there be no submission that there is no *prima facie* case against the defendant;
- no evidence be called by or on behalf of the defendant.

The evidence is not considered. The prosecutor having said that the case is ready for committal hands to the clerk the original witness statements and a copy thereof with a list of exhibits and any exhibits to be retained by the court. The clerk of the court then checks each witness statement and reads out the name of the witness at which point the defence and prosecution indicate whether they wish that witness to be fully or conditionally bound to appear in the Crown Court. The clerk then asks if the alibi warning (qv) is appropriate and if the prosecution deem it necessary (which will be in the majority of cases, as the defendant may change his solicitor or instructions) then it should be given in the following words 'You will be committed for trial by jury but I must warn you that you may not be permitted to give evidence of an alibi or to call witnesses in support of that alibi unless you have earlier given particulars of the alibi and of the witnesses. You or your solicitor may give those particulars now to this court or at any time in the next seven days to the solicitor for the prosecution'. The magistrates then commit the matter to the appropriate Crown Court with bail set as hitherto unless there are special circumstances. The defence will then apply for legal aid to be extended to the Crown Court.

2.5 Indictable offences

Indictable offences will advance to transfer or committal proceedings at the earliest opportunity and will be adjourned to the transfer hearing date, or adjourned at each appearance until enquiries are complete and the papers are ready.

2.6 Adjournment procedure

If an adjournment is granted then any witnesses may be called into court so that a mutually convenient date for proceeding can be set. The clerk will then indicate available dates and a date will be agreed. However, issues of bail may arise and dictate that the case be listed also for further remands on some other date before trial, sentencing or committal. This is discussed further in Chapter 3.

2.7 A timetable for proceedings in the magistrates' court

Proceedings should occur within a reasonable time of the offence so that there is no risk of prejudice to a defendant in the preparation or conduct of his defence. If the prosecution has manipulated or misused the process of the court, or there has been undue delay by the prosecution then the magistrates may exercise their powers to stop the prosecution as being vexatious or oppressive (POA 1985 s 22). However, regard should be given to the seriousness of the offence and proceedings for indictable offences should rarely be stopped (see *R v Oxford City Justices ex p Smith* (1982) 75 Cr App R 200).

There are few statutory time limits other than for appeals and the times given below are therefore solely guidelines based on experience. They are subject to local variation and negotiation with the Chief Metropolitan Magistrate.

2.7.1 Adjournments

The following times should be expected for adjournments:

Adjournment	*Time*
For printout (DVLC)	4 weeks
For committals	6 weeks or 4 weeks if defendant in custody
For reports	4 weeks or 3 weeks if defendant in custody
For analyses (drugs, blood, urine, etc)	up to 3 months
For advance information	2 weeks

2.7.2 Custody

Where the defendant is remanded in custody, he must come before the court within eight days of any previous appearance unless he agrees to be remanded in absence which remand will be to the next effective date such as committal, etc or for 28 days whichever is the shorter. After a guilty plea has been entered the maximum period allowed for any remand is four weeks. The maximum permissible period of remand in custody prior to summary trial or transfer/committal is 70 days (84 in Birmingham). After a mode of trial determination, there is a time limit of 56 days until summary trial. However, these limits can be extended on application, if the court is satisfied that there is good and sufficient cause for doing so or the prosecution has acted with all due expedition and is not at fault for the delay.

2.7.3 Summons

Information to be laid within six months of the alleged offence.

2.7.4 Service

Service of s 9 statements seven days prior to hearing.

2.7.5 Appeals

Within 21 days of the decision which is the subject of the appeal. Abandonment of appeal must be at least three working days before the date set for hearing.

2.8 Evidence

A full discussion of the rules of evidence is beyond the scope of this book. Particular matters to bear in mind and points of procedure alone are considered below. The majority of evidence is given orally and the general rules of evidence in criminal cases apply, eg as to exclusion of hearsay, etc. Certain written statements and written and oral admissions are also admissible by virtue of CJA 1967 ss 9, 10 or CJA 1988.

Evidence may not generally be called by any party after the close of that party's case. Unless the evidence is formal or arising *ex iprovisom*, eg in rebuttal, then the magistrates will not usually use their discretion to admit it.

2.8.1 Witnesses giving evidence

Witnesses giving evidence should wait outside court until called to give evidence. However, an exception arises for expert witnesses as in certain cases it may be in the interests of justice for them to hear all or part of the other evidence in the case. Outside court a witness is entitled to refresh his memory from his original statement (Stones Justices Manual 2.32), but he will not be able to refer to this in court unless this is a note made at the time of the incident such as a police officer's notebook or the statement is specifically referred to by the cross examining lawyer.

When witnesses are called into court they enter the witness box and are asked whether they wish to take the oath or affirm. Procedure varies according to the particular creed but once completed the witness is sworn and liable to be indicted for perjury if he states anything which he knows to be untrue. Children under the age of 14 must be asked whether they understand the nature of the oath and where they do not understand unsworn evidence may be taken (CYPA 1933 ss 28, 38, MCA 1980 s 102, CJA 1967 s 9). Note that by virtue of CJA 1988 s 34, such unsworn evidence in the absence of any corroboration may be sufficient for a conviction but caution in doing so is urged.

Once the witness has been sworn he will be introduced by the party calling them asking his name and address. If the witness is reluctant to disclose his address in open court then on furnishing adequate reasons, eg fear of reprisals, it may be sufficient for him to provide it written down for the magistrates. The witness will then usually be asked their occupation and, before being asked any specific questions, it is desirable to remind them to address their answers to the magistrates and inform them that a note is being taken so that they can give their evidence accordingly.

The examination in chief of witnesses should be conducted carefully ensuring as far as possible that all the points made in the witness' statement are covered whilst avoiding leading the witness. In the case of a witness giving evidence contrary to their initial statement, the party calling that witness may apply to have that witness deemed 'hostile' so that he may be cross examined on that statement and the changes (Archbold 4.305).

Police officers or store detectives are practised witnesses and will also have made a note of the incident to which they will wish to refer and in such cases one must introduce the notes. Specifically one should ask them or anyone else who has made such a note whether they took a note to which they wish to refer, when the note was taken, if that was the first available opportunity to do so and if the incident was fresh in their memory at that time. It is then up to the magistrates to decide whether the notes can be used. If used the notes should in principle be an *aide memoire* and should not be read directly. Other evidence which may be introduced in a similar manner are notes, for example, of a car registration plate taken at the scene of an incident by any witness (Stones Justices Manual 2.33).

The witness will then be cross examined by the opposing party during the course of which all challenges to the evidence should be put and any previous statements can be referred to. Re-examination then follows but must be restricted to matters arising out of cross examination and no fresh evidence can be called. The magistrates are then asked if they wish to ask any questions of the witness and should they do so they may invite the advocates to pursue that point.

Once the witness has concluded his evidence, the advocate calling that witness may ask the court if the witness can be released. If there are no objections and the magistrates agree, then the witness will be told that he can leave the precincts of the court but on doing so must not speak to any other person involved in the case.

2.8.2 Written statements and admissions

Written statements and written and oral admissions are admissible by virtue of CJA 1967 ss 9, 10 or CJA 1988. Written statements by witnesses can be produced in evidence provided that the conditions as set out in the CJA 1967 s 9 have been complied with, namely:

- that the statement purports to be signed by the person who made it;
- that it contains a declaration that it is true and that it has been made knowing that he would be liable to prosecution if he wilfully stated in it anything which he knew to be false;

- that, at least seven days prior to the hearing, a copy is served on the other parties to the proceedings; and
- that none of the other parties propose objecting to the statement.

The procedure for adducing s 9 statements is that the statement is introduced as having been served and accepted under the CJA 1967 s 9 and the original statement and a certificate of service is handed to the clerk. The witness' name, address and occupation is given and, after it has been said that the declaration has been made and the statement has been signed at the appropriate points at the head and foot of the page, the contents are read out.

Admissions of fact may be made and adduced as evidence for the purposes of any criminal proceedings by or on behalf of the prosecutor or the defendant by virtue of CJA 1967 s 10. It may be made before or at the proceedings but shall be in writing unless made in court. The court may ask for the admission to be put on a *pro forma* sheet or both parties should discuss and draft the admissions in an agreed statement. In either event, the document is signed by defence and prosecution and introduced by one of them as appropriate.

2.8.3 Other admissible evidence

Documents and statements from certain unavailable witnesses (such as those abroad or deceased) can also be admitted as evidence as well as, *inter alia*, computer records, plans, photographs, tapes, videos, etc subject to the statutory safeguards. The law on documentary evidence was clarified by the CJA 1988, and documents may be admitted in certain cases (CJA 1988 ss 23, 28). The same Act abolished the requirement for corroboration of the unsworn evidence of a child for conviction of an offender, and made several other provisions relating to evidence in criminal proceedings (CJA 1988 ss 29–34).

2.8.4 Exclusion of evidence

The magistrates are triers of fact and law in the magistrates' court. Any questions of law as to admissibility are, therefore, decided by the magistrates with the assistance of the justices' clerk and the advocates. As far as possible, such questions should be broached at the earliest opportunity, and can be discussed with the opposing representative prior to the hearing. If the issue is fundamental then it should be put before any evidence is called and other points put as they arise.

3 Sentencing

In determining sentence magistrates are required to consider a number of factors including matters of practice, policy and statute, including the rehabilitation of offenders, which combine with factors peculiar to each case to make this a tricky matter. Certain of these matters are laid out below, and others will usually be contained in the social inquiry reports prepared for them, the facts of the case and the plea in mitigation. In all cases the magistrates are bound by the general principles of sentencing, eg 'the seriousness test' under CJA 1991 s 1(2) in relation to a custodial sentence and s 6(1) in relation to a community sentence, the relevance of previous convictions under CJA 1991 s 29 and other provisions in relation to length of sentence and aggregation of offences in determining such periods. The practitioner should consult a specialist sentencing work for this background and also refer to the magistrates' own 'bible' – the Magistrates' Association Sentencing Guidelines – which designate an 'entry point' on the scale of seriousness for an offence of an 'average' nature and precise suggested variations on a sliding scale for offences with aggravated or mitigating factors.

3.1 Powers

The powers of magistrates' courts set out in the Magistrates' Court Act 1980 ss 31, 32 and 133(2) limit the court to imposing no more than six months imprisonment for any one offence and a maximum fine of £5,000. Where they are dealing with two or more 'either way' offences (excluding criminal damage to a total under £5,000) consecutive sentences may be given to a total of 12 months imprisonment. Within these powers the magistrates' court is further limited by various provisions notably in relation to young offenders, ie those under 21. Sentencing options for those under 21 are separately listed. The Powers of Criminal Courts Act 1973 defines and expresses some of these options. Further rules were also contained in the Criminal Justice Act 1988 and are included below.

3.2 Procedure

After a guilty plea the prosecutor will outline the facts of the offence to the court and introduce any offences taken into consideration, make any appropriate ancillary applications (eg costs, compensation, destruction or forfeiture orders) and put the defendant's antecedents (previous convictions which he has agreed with the defendant). If the defendant pleaded not guilty then the summary of the offence is omitted unless it is a matter which has been adjourned for sentence.

Offences taken into consideration may include any offences even if the defendant has not been formally charged with them or other offences related to the instant offence (Stones Justices Manual 3.26). These offences are noted on a form prepared for the purpose, signed by the defendant to acknowledge his admission and handed to the clerk for reading out. No offences can be so entered if there has been pressure on the defendant or if the magistrates would not have jurisdiction to hear them. Offences of a different nature may be included, save if they are likely to present difficulties in sentencing such as if there is introduced the possibility of disqualification, different types of dishonesty or breach of probation, etc.

Once the prosecution has completed the introduction to the case the defendant or his representative is invited to speak in mitigation of the offence, although this may not be necessary on the first appearance when the court may have indicated that it will be asking for reports, or counsel asks them to do so and they concur.

As mentioned above, the magistrates may decide to adjourn the matter so that reports (including social inquiry, medical or psychiatric reports) can be prepared, or it may be incumbent on them to do so. In the absence of a submission by the defence for such reports, magistrates have no general duty to ask for them if they consider them unnecessary. However, where they are thinking of a custodial sentence for any juvenile or an adult who has not previously received a custodial sentence, reports are usually obtained and, in any instance where magistrates impose a custodial sentence without reports, they are required to state in open court their reasons for doing so.

Alternatively, or in addition, the magistrates may ask for a community service assessment, ie an assessment to be made as to whether the defendant would be suitable for community service. Having heard the mitigation and reports, if prepared, the magistrates will then either retire to arrive at a sentence (Stones Justice Manual 3.23).

3.3 Sentencing options – general

By the Acts mentioned above the various options available are those listed below. Fines can be imposed in addition to any other sentence, and ancillary orders of compensation, forfeiture, etc can be imposed in certain cases defined by the statute creating them for which reference should be made to Chapter 7.

3.3.1 Imprisonment, suspended, concurrent or consecutive, part suspension

Imprisonment should not be imposed on anyone who has not previously been sentenced to a period of imprisonment unless there is no other appropriate method of dealing with them. It is also not an option for anyone under the age of 21 who may only be sentenced to detention in a young offender institution.

Suspended sentences should not be passed unless immediate imprisonment would be appropriate in the absence of a power to suspend (PCCA 1973 s 22). They are also now limited to cases where there are 'exceptional circumstances' (CJA 1989). The period of the suspension or operational period must be at least one but no more than two years. Before passing the sentence the court must explain the consequences of a breach of it.

Part suspended sentences of imprisonment may be passed by the court with respect to any sentence of not less than three months; the part to be served immediately must be not less than 28 days or more than three quarters of the total. The operational period of the suspended part of the sentence is the period between release and the date on which he would without remission be released were the sentence not part suspended (CLA 1977 s 47 amended by CJA 1982 s 30).

3.3.2 Deferred sentence

The court may, with the defendant's consent, defer passing sentence for up to six months for the purpose of assessing the defendant's conduct and any change in his circumstances. The defendant is then sentenced at the end of the deferment period, and when he reappears to be sentenced the court may then pass any sentence which the deferring court could have passed including a committal to the Crown Court. If the defendant has not committed any offence and his conduct is satisfactory he should not ordinarily be sent to prison when sentenced.

3.3.3 Community service order

The community service order (PCCA 1973 ss 14–17) is made as an alternative to other sentences and principally as an alternative to imprisonment, youth custody or detention centre. Before considering this course the court will usually ask for an assessment of suitability, to consider the defendant's talents, and whether he can make himself available.

An offender must be over 16. The maximum period for any sentence of community service is 240 hours (or 120 hours if the offender is under 17) and the minimum is 40 hours. Sentences of community service can be made consecutive or concurrent but if consecutive the total sentence must not exceed 240 hours (120 for a 16 year old).

Before passing a sentence of community service the court must have considered a probation report and be satisfied that the defendant is suitable and the defendant must consent to the order. The work is usually done under the direction of a probation officer and should be completed within 12 months without interfering with the defendant's school or work or religious beliefs.

3.3.4 Probation order

Probation orders (PCCA 1973 ss 2–13) can be made on any offender over 17 as an alternative to sentencing for the offence. Such orders must be made for a period of at least six months and no more than three years. They can only be made with the offender's consent, the effect of the order having been explained to him. Conditions which may be attached include:

- residence at a probation hostel;
- treatment for a mental condition where such condition has been identified by a duly qualified practitioner and does not warrant the making of an hospital order;
- attendance at a day centre or specified activities for a period not exceeding 60 days, such requirement only to be included after consultation with a probation officer; and
- restraint from specified activities.

Orders are then supervised by a probation officer appointed to the area of the supervising court.

3.3.5 Fines

Fines are available as a penalty for any offence but must be considered in the light of other penalties, orders for costs and compensation. They can be ordered paid from any money in the possession of the offender at arrest or a search of the offender may be ordered at court.

The maximum fine for an offender over 18 years is £5,000 or the amount in the statute if less. For an offender under 14 years the maximum fine is £250, and for an offender over 14 but under 18 years the maximum is £1,000. Maximum fines for any offence are now set on a single scale which was amended by the CJA 1988 and may be updated from time to time by the Home Secretary. Sections 51–54 of the Act give guidelines for converting references in other legislation to amounts on the standard scale. Offences triable either way are subject to the statutory maximum.

Scale of maximum fines on conviction for a summary offence

Scale	*Fine*
Level 1	£200
Level 2	£500
Level 3	£1,000
Level 4	£2,500
Level 5	£5,000

As a broad guide monetary penalties should normally be such that the offender can pay within about 12 months, his means being put to the court in the mitigation (including outgoings such as rent, mortgage, dependants' living costs) and an offer as to the mode of payment being made once the amount has been set. Some courts use a unit system in dealing with fines (although this is no longer required by statute), where one unit is the weekly disposable income of an offender (or £100 if this is less). In either case, the court may make a financial circumstances order requiring the offender to provide a statement of means to help with the financial assessment, but may proceed without this information if the offender has been convicted in his absence, failed to comply with the financial circumstances order, or in any other way hindered the court's inquiries.

In the case of offenders under 16, the court must order the parent or guardian to pay the fine unless this would be unreasonable in the circumstances of the case. In the case of offenders aged 16 or 17, the court has a power to order the parent to pay if it is not unreasonable to do so.

If the fine has not been paid by the set date then the defendant may be required to appear at a means inquiry and sentenced to imprisonment for non payment.

Maximum imprisonment in default of payment of fines

Fine		*Imprisonment*
Amount not exceeding	£200	7 days
	£500	14 days
	£1,000	28 days
	£2,500	45 days
	£5,000	3 months
	£10,000	6 months
Amounts in excess of	£10,000	12 months

3.3.6 Discharge

The conditional or absolute discharge is an order made by the court where it is of the opinion that it is inexpedient to inflict punishment and a probation order is inappropriate (PCCA 1973 s 7) and are given in limited cases only.

3.3.7 Breach of orders

Breach of a conditional discharge by a defendant may result in sentencing for both the original offence and the next offence. Breach of probation orders, or community service orders may result in a fine, or the court dealing with the offender for the original offence, or if the order was made by the Crown Court he may be committed to that court for that court to deal with the breach.

3.3.8 Other penalties

Disqualification from driving and endorsements can be imposed for appropriate offences involving motor vehicles as well as road traffic offences. If disqualification is imposed with imprisonment the period should not be excessive, for reasons of rehabilitation and for the practical reason that driving whilst disqualified may result (*R v West* [1986] 8 Cr App R (S) 266).

Binding over orders require an individual to enter into a recognisance, sometimes with a surety, to be of good behaviour and/or to keep the peace for a fixed period of time, usually one or two years. The power to bind over is not confined to binding the defendant or to the end of the trial and is considered principally as preventative justice. Further detail on the procedure and practice is given in Chapter 6. Exclusion orders, precluding offenders from licensed premises or football matches and restriction orders preventing offenders from travelling abroad are also available in certain circumstances.

3.4 Sentencing of juveniles/persons under 21

Provisions for sentencing of juveniles have been extensively modified in the CJA 1988 which amalgamated the previous custodial sentences of youth custody and detention in a detention centre to a single possible sentence of detention in a young offender institution. Any of the non custodial sentences is available to the court, except that for probation an offender must be over 17. For community service an offender must be over 16 and if under 17 the maximum term is 120 hours rather than 240 hours. The Criminal Justice and Public Order Act 1994 also introduced a new sentence, the secure training order, for offenders aged 12–14. This is an entirely new sentence, being a period of detention followed by a period of supervision. It applies where the offender has committed an imprisonable offence after the age of 12 plus three other imprisonable offences, one of which was in breach of a supervision order: CJPOA 1994 s 1. Interim arrangements are to be made with local authorities when separate secure training order facilities become available.

3.4.1 Detention in a young offender institution

Detention orders are available as an alternative sentence on any male offender over 14 but under 21 and any female offender over 15 but under 21. They must have been convicted of an imprisonable offence and the court must consider that:

- the circumstances, including the nature and gravity of the offence, are such that if the offender were over 21 a sentence of imprisonment would be imposed; and
- the offender qualifies for a custodial sentence.

The latter condition is met if:

- he has a history of failing to respond to non custodial penalties and is unable or unwilling to do so; or

- only a custodial sentence would be adequate to protect the public from harm; or
- the offence is so serious that a non custodial sentence cannot be justified.

The minimum term is 21 days but if the offender is a female under 17 she shall not be given a sentence whose effect is that she would be sentenced to a total term of four months or less. The maximum sentence for an offender under 15 is four months and if a sentence is made consecutive to any other such order then the total period should not exceed four months. For an offender aged 15 or over the maximum is 12 months (six months for any offence in the magistrates' court but subject to a total of 12 months). The physical and mental condition of the offender must be considered and the order must not be made if the offender has served or is serving any sentence of imprisonment, borstal training, youth custody or detention under CYPA 1933 s 53.

3.4.2 Attendance orders

Attendance at an Attendance Centre may be ordered for any offender under 21 convicted of an imprisonable offence (CJA 1982 ss 16–19). Hours must be not less than 12 (except for offenders under 14 if 12 hours seems excessive) and not more than 36 (24 if the offender is less than 17). Attendance orders should not be made if previous custodial sentences have been served unless there are special circumstances.

3.4.3 Committal for sentence

Committal for sentence from the magistrates' court to the Crown Court is available as an alternative under MCA 1980 s 38 if on hearing details of the antecedents and character of a defendant over 17 the justices are of the opinion that he merits greater punishment than they have power to give. Committal should not, therefore, be used solely because the case is more serious than was first thought. By CJA 1982 s 63 committal is still allowed after sentence has been deferred.

By MCA 1980 s 37 a juvenile, that is a person who is not less than 15 nor more than 16 years old, may be committed to the Crown Court for sentence in respect of a conviction on indictment if the magistrates' court is of the opinion that he should be sentenced to a greater term of youth custody than it has power to impose. The Crown Court can then impose a youth custody sentence not exceeding 12 months (CJA

1982 s 7(1), (8)) but powers of extended sentence under CYPA 1933 s 53(2) are not available.

Additional provisions relating to committal for sentence are found in CJA 1967 s 56, Powers of Criminal Act 1973 ss 8(6) and 24(2) and the Bail Act 1976 s 6(6).

3.4.4 Ancillary orders

Compensation

PCCA 1973 ss 35-38. Instead of or in addition to any other sentence a court may order an offender to pay compensation for any personal injury, loss or damage resulting from the offence or any offence taken into consideration up to a limit of £5,000 per offence. Compensation can not be ordered for loss suffered by dependants through the death of the victim (rarely an issue in the magistrates' court) of an offence or for loss, injury or damage arising out of the presence of a motor vehicle on a road. It is accorded precedence over any fine for the offence. The sum must be agreed by the defendant or otherwise be proved by way of invoices subject to argument.

Forfeiture

PCCA 1973 s 43. Forfeiture may be ordered only when a person is convicted of an indictable offence punishable with imprisonment for two years or more. The section only operates to deprive a defendant of any rights in any property which the court is satisfied was in his possession or control at the time of his apprehension and was used for committing or facilitating an offence. Once forfeited the item may be destroyed (as with drugs, weapons etc) or sold, or may later be claimed by the owner if not involved in the crime.

Restitution of stolen goods

TA 1968 s 28. Restitution of stolen goods may be ordered at the court's own initiative of property which is the subject of an offence under the Theft Acts 1968 and 1978, or any such offences taken into consideration. Alternatively, the offender may be ordered to make a payment from any money found in his possession when he is arrested.

Deportation

Deportation can be ordered of any person who is not a British citizen if they are over 17 and have been convicted of an offence punishable with imprisonment. In deciding whether to make a recommendation for deportation, the court should consider whether the offender's continued presence in the UK would be detrimental (taking account of the seriousness of the crime, his criminal record etc) and the effect on other innocent persons such as his family. Excluded from consideration at this stage are the consequences to the offender of being returned to his own country, this being a matter for the Home Secretary. The procedure is that there should be a full enquiry into the case before a recommendation is made, the defendant having been given seven clear days notice. He should have legal aid and be represented.

Binding over of parents

Parents may be required to enter into a recognisance to take proper care of a juvenile under 16 if the court thinks that would help the juvenile to refrain from committing further offences. The court must state its reactions if it does *not* avail itself of this power where it could do so: CJA 1991 s 58.

3.5 Mental health provisions

3.5.1 Hospital order (Mental Health Act 1983)

On conviction of an offence punishable by imprisonment the court may order the offender to be detained in hospital or, by a guardianship order, to be placed under the control of the local social services under the Mental Health Act 1983 s 37 if, on the evidence of two properly qualified medical practitioners, it is satisfied that he is suffering from mental illness, psychopathic disorder or mental impairment and that either:

- the nature and degree of the disorder makes it appropriate for him to be detained and, in the case of psychopathic disorder or mental impairment, treatment would alleviate or prevent deterioration of his condition; or
- for an offender over 16, the mental condition is of a nature or degree which warrants his reception into guardianship, and the court is of the opinion that in all the circumstances such an order is the most suitable way of dealing with an offence.

The order should not be made unless there is evidence that the defendant can be received into the specified hospital within 28 days. In the interim, he may be detained in a place of safety as defined in MHA 1983 s 5. Hospital orders may also be appropriate where the defendant is unfit to plead (qv).

Sentencing practice

Sentence	*Age of offender (years)*						
	10–13	*14**	*14***	*15*	*16*	*17–21*	*over 21*
Imprisonment							✓
Suspended/partly suspended							✓
Young offenders institution			✓	✓	✓	✓	
Community service order					✓	✓	✓
Attendance centre	✓	✓	✓	✓	✓	✓	
Hospital order	✓	✓	✓	✓	✓	✓	✓
Guardianship order	✓	✓	✓	✓	✓	✓	✓
Fine	✓	✓	✓	✓	✓	✓	✓
Compensation order	✓	✓	✓	✓	✓	✓	✓
Probation order						✓	✓
Discharge	✓	✓	✓	✓	✓	✓	✓
Committal for sentence				✓	✓	✓	✓
Deferred sentence	✓	✓	✓	✓	✓	✓	✓

* Male

** Female

4 Bail

Bail is the release from a police station or the court of a defendant subject to a duty to surrender to custody at a later date. If bail is not granted the defendant is detained in custody. The issue of bail can arise at any appearance of the defendant in a magistrates' court until the conclusion of his case following any decision to adjourn the matter. It may also arise if the defendant fails to appear and a warrant is issued. The magistrates will then consider whether the warrant should be backed for bail, ie whether the defendant should have bail when arrested on that warrant or be detained in custody. The court further has a duty to consider granting bail on any application. The granting of bail is principally governed by the Bail Act 1976 and the Bail (Amendment) Act 1993, and CJPOA 1994.

Arriving in court for the first time the defendant will either have been held in custody by police officers or have been given bail to attend (PACEA 1984 s 38). If the defendant's case is not completed on his first appearance then the question of bail will arise. The determination of bail at this stage is entirely separate from the decision arrived at by police officers although the same considerations apply.

If the case is to be adjourned then the prosecution give the objections to bail within the terms of Bail Act 1976 s 4 set out in Sched 1 thereof, namely:

- that the defendant would fail to surrender to custody;
- that he may commit other offences whilst on bail;
- that he may interfere with witnesses or otherwise obstruct the course of justice;
- that it is necessary for his own protection or welfare;
- that he is already serving a custodial sentence;
- if the court is satisfied that it is impracticable to obtain the information necessary to determine the matter;
- if he has already been bailed in the course of these proceedings and been arrested as an absconder.

In support of these objections the prosecution may adduce information available such as previous convictions, the known personal circumstances of the defendant and details of the alleged offence. Previous convictions must be agreed by the defendant and can be verified by a fingerprint check if necessary (CJA 1948 s 39). However, by CJPOA 1994 s 25 bail may be refused if the defendant is charged with, or has previously been convicted of, murder or attempted murder, manslaughter (if a custodial sentence was received) or rape or attempted rape. By s 26 bail need not be granted if the offence charged is indictable or triable either way and the defendant was on bail already at the date of the alleged offence.

The defendant or his representative can then address the court to answer the objections. In the course of this the defence can propose that the objections can be met by imposing conditions of bail, eg residence, curfew, sureties, reporting to a police station etc and each point made by the prosecution argued. However, before opposing objections, full instructions should be taken and it might be wise to wait until one is in a stronger position with respect to meeting the objections. Alternatively, the magistrates may not deem the application full, particularly if this is the defendant's first appearance in court after being arrested the previous day.

The court will then decide the issue of bail taking into account matters raised by both sides from the standpoint that bail is a right of the defendant. A certificate is then issued which must give details if bail is refused: BA 1976 s 5(3). This is to assist the defendant to decide whether to apply for bail again, to the same court or elsewhere, ie to the Crown Court or High Court. If the offence is not imprisonable bail will only be withheld if the defendant has failed to comply with conditions of bail in the past and the court considers that he would fail to surrender to custody or he is already in custody or should be kept in custody for his own protection or it is necessary so that reports can be compiled (BA 1976 s 7).

Where bail conditional on a surety is granted, that surety may be taken at a police station or at court. If the surety is taken at court the procedure is that the suretor is called by the defence and gives his name and address, then is asked if he understands the requirement of him. He is then asked if, and how, he can raise the sum proposed as a surety and if the court is satisfied on this it asks if there are any police objections to the suretor before certifying bail.

Applications for bail can be entered at each appearance in the magistrates' court but, in general, after two applications, it must be shown that there has been a significant change in the defendant's circumstances for bail to be granted. In the event of a denial of bail the defendant may appeal to a judge in chambers in the Crown Court (Bail Act 1976 s 5 and Supreme Court Act 1981 s 81) or to the High Court. If the defendant is not represented the magistrates must inform him of these rights. The Bail (Amendment) Act 1993 permits the prosecution to appeal against the grant of bail by the magistrates where the defendant is charged with or convicted of an offence punishable by imprisonment of five years or more, or an offence under s 12 or s 12A of the Theft Act 1968. However, in order to invoke this right the prosecution must object to the grant of bail *before* it was granted: s 1(1). However, s 30 of the Act creates s 5A of BA 1976 permitting the prosecution to apply to have bail revoked, or conditions attached to it, when new information comes to light *after* bail was granted. (This only applies to indictable or either way offences.)

4.1 Time limits

If the defendant is remanded in custody or on bail, there are statutory limits on the maximum period of remand at one time (MCA 1980 ss 5, 6, 10, 18, 37, 38, 128–31). For adults these are:

- three clear days remand in the custody of a constable before conviction;
- eight clear days remand in custody to a prison department establishment before conviction, unless the offence is triable either way and is to be tried summarily and a court can not be properly constituted in that time;
- three weeks remand in custody after conviction for inquiries or reports;
- four weeks remand on bail after conviction for inquiries or reports,
- any period to which prosecution and defence agree for remand on bail prior to conviction;
- 28 clear days remand in custody before conviction, of a person who still has at least that to serve as a custodial sentence;
- until appearance at the Crown Court, when committed for trial or sentence.

Bail pending appeal against conviction or sentence can be granted by the magistrates' court, or by the appellate court. The latter may be preferred as it is less likely that the court having made the determination complained of will grant the application. In principle, the prosecution require 24 hours notice of an application but in exceptional circumstances they may waive such notice. Note that the defendant may choose not to appear at any remand date, and be remanded in custody in his absence for a further period of up to eight days, but he can only be so remanded to a maximum of 28 days.

4.2 Checklist for answering bail objections

Objection	*Answer*
Failing to attend	Residence (bail hostel)
Past record of failing to attend	Local ties (family, mortgage, job)
Seriousness of offence, strength of evidence	Sureties, reporting to police station
Commit further offences, likely sentence	Sureties
Past record (frequency) of offences	Curfew, condition to avoid certain locations (eg streets, public transport, etc)
Interfere with witnesses	Curfew, condition of residence and avoidance of certain locations Condition not to approach or otherwise interfere with prosecution witnesses
Own protection or welfare	Available accommodation (hospital) Welfare or voluntary assistance, family support

5 Advocacy practice

The focus of this chapter is to give some assistance primarily to those entering this arena for the first time, and provide checklists for those occasions when one needs it. There are, nonetheless, some points which advocates in general should bear in mind. The first is that one's duty is twofold: to ensure that the court is not misled, and the second to submit the client's case in the most effective and advantageous manner. In doing so, one should be courteous to all court staff as well as one's opponent and the magistrates. Thereafter personal appearance is important in creating a favourable impression for oneself and one's client, whilst attention should be paid to method of presentation and professional standards.

Magistrates, and most clients, prefer to see sober dress and grooming in court whereas informal attire may give the impression of a casual approach to the matter in hand. An attractive, dignified and poised manner in court is equally important and an aggressive attitude to witnesses, magistrates or court staff is usually counterproductive to one's case whether defending or prosecuting. Magistrates are given a certain amount of discretion and are unlikely to exercise that discretion in favour of one who is discourteous, and fails to apologise if late for court or absent when the case is called or is otherwise offensive. Magistrates should be addressed as Sir or Madam, addressing the whole bench as if they were the chairman or chairwoman alone.

The presentation of a case should be clear, in elocution and in understanding. This aspect of a case requires preparation, and repetition of half remembered authorities will not impress or persuade the lay magistrate. Cases should be cited properly in full giving page and paragraph numbers for any quote used, and the court's attention should be drawn to all relevant cases including those possibly adverse to one's client's interests. Some courts request that cases to be cited are made available well in advance of the hearing, but this is not a general requirement. The *dicta* should not be given without the facts and *ratio* so that the court is aware of the relevance of that *dictum*. Textbook writers only become authorities, strictly speaking, posthumously and if the writer is living his writing should be incorporated in one's submissions and not referred to as an authority. However, in practice, certain textbooks, eg Archbold, the White Book and Wilkinson are cited as authorities.

The date of publication of any text referred to should be given.

Factors which will aid preparation of a case are given below. In court the prosecution should endeavour to present the case fairly and quietly. The defendant is allowed a certain amount more vigour but with realism, without posturing (political or otherwise) and with integrity.

5.1 Prosecuting

The task of prosecuting in the magistrates' court has been a function of the Crown Prosecution Service (CPS) since the Prosecution of Offences Act 1985. It is CPS policy to use solicitors and barristers as agents to present cases as well as their own staff, and on any particular day a prosecutor may be asked to conduct anything from a single trial or committal to an entire remand list or traffic court. Those working for the Crown Prosecution Service will be trained in and aware of CPS practice, so that much of the following chapter is addressed primarily to those undertaking prosecution for the first time.

General instructions to agents are given by the individual branches of the CPS and should be read in addition to any specific instructions on a case. Issued with these instructions is further information on matters such as endorsement of the files using computer codes or expenses and costs etc. The necessity to apply for costs should be borne in mind by the prosecutor at the conclusion of any case.

5.1.1 The CPS file

The CPS file consists of an outer jacket which carries all endorsements relating to court proceedings inside of which is a folder of correspondence and a bundle of case papers contained within a form prepared on the case by the police. This form, properly completed, should give most of the information necessary to present the case. On the first page is found the name of the defendant, the charge and the anticipated plea. Then there will be an indication as to whether ancillary orders are to be sought, eg compensation, forfeiture, destruction. If an adjournment is sought on behalf of the prosecution brief reasons as to why this is necessary should be stated although in cases of any complexity it is often advisable and helpful to the court if the officer in the case can attend. There is also an indication as to the names of witnesses and their available dates on this page.

On the inside front cover will be found a brief *precis* of the relevant facts though this should be relied on solely as a guide to the case and not a definitive introduction thereto. Sometimes background information on the case or the defendant is added at the foot of this page, eg the relative builds of assailant and victim or a medical history.

The inside back cover has personal details, specifically nationality, marital, domestic and financial circumstances (if the defendant has chosen to give them). Also given is the Criminal Records Office (CRO) number, if any, to indicate that the defendant has previous convictions. In any event, the agent should check whether there is a form giving details of convictions separately within the bundle and/or a printout from DVLC Swansea in any driving matters. Previous convictions should always be confirmed in advance with the defendant or verified by fingerprint checks performed by police officers, if disputed (CJA 1948 s 39). Unconfirmed convictions should not then be put before the court but the matter can usually be put back to give time for the checks to be done.

On the back cover there is space for a summary of confirmed or unconfirmed previous convictions which should be relied on only if there is no form 609. There is also an indication as to whether there are other proceedings pending and, if so, the conditions of bail attached. In addition, the form states the police view as to whether unconditional bail can be granted. If there are police objections these should be supported by the inclusion in the bundle of a further form detailing the reasons for seeking a remand in custody or the imposition of conditions. A further discussion of bail is given separately.

5.2 Prosecution checklist

- Prosecution bundle
- Form giving case details prepared by investigating officer
- Form detailing previous convictions (at least four copies: magistrates, clerk, defence and file copy)
- Charge sheet
- Bail form statements, including originals and extra copies at committals
- Other evidence, eg breathalyser readout, DVLC printout
- Deportation form (if needed)
- Advance information documents (where appropriate)
- Compensation claim form (if appropriate)

- Check charges and prefer all charges at first available opportunity
- Check category of offence for either way offences, determine the gravity of the offence and preferred mode of trial
- Check file to ensure that full facts are available so that any determination can be made in the light of those facts, eg medical evidence of injuries and full list of stolen goods, etc
- Alibi warnings (at committals)
- Bail conditions (if any)

On arrival at court check for any extra cases or overnight charges for the court in question, and endeavour to liaise with the defence as far as possible to aid presentation of cases in court (eg so that one is aware whether any adjournment is to be applied for, if a guilty plea is to be entered, etc).

In court, after the magistrates' entry, the defendant will be called and the prosecutor should open by stating the stage of proceedings in the case, ie first appearance, if advance information has been served, or if the prosecution is seeking an adjournment for any reason. Thereafter, proceedings vary according to the case in question and Chapter 2 gives details of this.

Opening speeches should be short but outline events clearly so that the magistrates can follow the evidence thereafter, and should describe the elements of the alleged offence. The prosecution has no closing speech and, therefore, they must endeavour to present their case in total at the first opportunity and should open all cases even if relatively simple. Individual witnesses can be referred to but detail of their evidence should be avoided.

5.3 Defending

When defending, the first priority is to take full instructions from the client and give advice accordingly. Matters of administration such as attending to legal aid should also be completed before court and much court time and effort can be saved by liasing with the CPS to ascertain what, if any, bail objections there are and other relevant details. Thereafter, proceedings will depend on the case in question and one's instructions, the treatment of which will be a matter of individual judgment.

In court, proceedings will be commenced by the prosecution as outlined above. Thereafter, unless one is asking for advance information or there is a specific reason for an adjournment application at this stage, the procedure is as outlined in Chapter 2.

At the end of a summary trial the defence advocate may make a closing speech, which some practitioners prepare in advance of their examinations in chief or cross examinations amending as necessary. The speech should concentrate on the evidence presented and attempt to show how this is insufficient to discharge the burden of proof or, alternatively, how an element of the offence has not been proved. No new evidence can be included. If any law is involved then the statute and any supporting cases should be cited, and copies thereof provided for the magistrates, the prosecution and the clerk as far as possible.

After a guilty verdict or plea, the defence advocate will be called on to mitigate. Mitigation is a singular art and possibly the most important function of an advocate in the magistrates' court. On occasion one should spend as much time on preparing one's mitigation as one might on the rest of a case, and the satisfaction from putting a good plea in mitigation can be as rewarding as any verdict.

In mitigation, matters which are admitted should be stated frankly and events mitigated as far as is possible but avoid trying to describe a crime as trivial or forwarding a defence. The offence having been dealt with, the circumstances of the offender should be outlined.

Mitigating factors which should be forwarded are firstly the background to the offence, the family background of the offender and his personal and financial position. Contrition, including any recompense already made, should be mentioned, if possible, but avoided if the defendant has pleaded not guilty.

Reports should be referred to when they have been prepared but care should be exercised when conclusions are discussed as some magistrates have the view that lenient sentences are often recommended. One's own recommendation of sentence for consideration by the magistrates can and should be put with a coherent argument to back it up. Such argument should stress any previous good character, work record and future consequences of a penalty, and if backed with authority has increased persuasiveness though the magistrates need not be bound by authority alone and one might close with a general plea for leniency.

5.4 Defence checklist

- Brief identifying defendant
- Full instructions including details as to residence, employment, family circumstances, possible sureties
- Means – income including benefit etc and all outgoings, eg bills, mortgage payments, HP payments

- Character references, work references
- Witnesses, including those who might support mitigation
- Legal aid, advance information or committal papers (if appropriate)
- List of previous convictions, copy of social inquiry report (if available) from the court probation officer
- Driving licence, insurance certificate, etc (for appropriate cases)

6 Alternative procedures

6.1 Binding over

Binding over is an order made by magistrates requiring a defendant to enter into a recognisance to keep the peace for a certain period. The Justices of the Peace Act 1361 gives to magistrates the power to bind over any person appearing before them at any stage of the proceedings without the necessity for formal complaint or a full hearing. They may also exercise the power at common law or by virtue of the MCA 1980 s 115. Additionally, under CYPA 1969 s 7(7) the parent or guardian of a child or young person found guilty of an offence before any court may be ordered to enter into a recognisance to take proper care of him and to exercise proper control.

The intention of such orders is 'preventative justice' and not punishment but an order may be made in addition to any sentence should it be considered appropriate. A common use of binding over orders by magistrates in recent times is in scenes of minor public disorder, eg neighbourhood disputes or non violent demonstrations. In such cases, the prosecution will often agree to offer no evidence against the defendant if he agrees to be bound over and no conviction is then recorded. Alternatively, it may be that the justices feel that further such disturbances will be prevented by such an order and may bind over any of the parties appearing before them.

The procedure for binding over must be strictly observed. Where the prosecution is offering no evidence upon agreement of the defendant to be bound, the procedure is that the prosecutor will stand and state that subject to the court's discretion the matter could be disposed of by means of a bind over. An outline of the case and evidence is put before the court and on this evidence the court must consider that unless a bind over is imposed there might be a future breach of the peace. The defence may then be called to make representations and, if a bind over is appropriate, address the court as to the defendant's means so that an appropriate recognisance can be determined. The defendant then enters into the recognisance which is put to him by the magistrates in a set form of words.

The issue of a bind over may also arise by way of complaint and by MCA 1980 s 115. If a complaint is made by any individual who fears physical harm, or that a breach of the peace is likely, and the complaint is held to be true, then a party refusing to be bound as required will be liable to be committed to custody for a period not exceeding six months or until the order is complied with.

The penalty for breach of a binding over order is forfeiture of all or part of the recognisance only, and no further penalty can be imposed. Justices have no power to attach conditions to the order (*Ayu* (1959) 43 Cr App R 31 and *Randall* (1986) 8 Cr App R (S) 433). Exercise of the power must be judicious and not contrary to natural justice.

An individual is required to enter into the recognisance and acknowledge themselves so bound. However, the penalty for a juvenile at common law who refuses to do so has not been resolved since CJA 1982 which abolished imprisonment for persons under 21. Appeals against binding over may be to the High Court for judicial review or the Crown Court. There is no maximum or minimum period to the power but one or two years is usual.

6.2 Contempt of court

Wilful insult of the justices, any witness or officer of the court at court, or going to or returning from the court, as well as wilful interruption of the proceedings and other misbehaviour constitutes contempt of court. This may be dealt with by the magistrate by virtue of s 12 of the Contempt of Court Act 1981. It is also contempt of court by virtue of s 9 of the same Act to use in court (or bring into court for use) a tape recorder or other instrument for recording sound without the leave of the court, or to publish a recording of legal proceedings thus made, or use any recording made in court other than in accordance with the conditions imposed by the court.

The court may order that the offender be taken into custody until the rising of the court, or be committed to prison for up to one month or fined or both. Alternatively, he may be bound over (qv). Persons under the age of 17 may not be committed to custody and those between 17 and 20 years may only be committed to detention (or youth custody) if there is no other appropriate method of dealing with them. A committal order may at any time be revoked by the magistrates' of their own motion or on application by the defendant. Committal should only be used where it is urgent and imperative to do so as anyone disrupting court may simply be ordered to leave.

In determining the issue of contempt of court, the court must be satisfied beyond reasonable doubt that the offence is made out. The court may decide that they could deal with the case at once but it is suggested that natural justice would provide for the allegation to be put to the offender and that he may be legally represented but, if proceedings are adjourned there is no power to remand in custody or on bail. Appeal against contempt of court is to the Crown Court but only in respect of the order made. The finding of contempt is nonetheless subject to judicial review.

7 Principal offences

Principal offences are listed in this chapter with details of mode of trial and maximum sentencing limits in the magistrates' court. Additional space is provided for notes on elements of the offence, case law and sentencing guidelines. Aiding and abetting an offence is charged as if for the full offence. Attempting an indictable offence is charged by virtue of the Criminal Attempts Act 1981 s 1, and it should be borne in mind that the attempting of an offence which would have been impossible to complete on the particular facts is nonetheless an offence. CAA s 3 covers other attempts. The sentencing limits and mode of trial for attempt are the same as for the full offence.

Table of principal offences

Act	*Offence*	*Mode of trial*[1]	*Max fine*[2]	*Max imprisonment*	*Elements*
CAA 1981	Vehicle interference (s 9)	S	4	3 months	Intention to steal vehicle or trailer or steal therein or to drive it away without authority
Criminal Damage Act 1971	• Threat to destroy	E	5	6 months	
	• Criminal damage	E[3]	5	6 months	Reckless or intentional damage
	• Possession with intent to destroy	E	5	6 months	
Customs and Excise Management Act 1979	Customs and excise duty evasion	E	5[4]	6 months	
CJA 1967	Drunk and disorderly	S	3	—	Public place
CJA 1988	Pointed instrument	S	3	—	Public place without excuse

Act	*Offence*	*Mode of trial*[1]	*Max fine*[2]	*Max imprisonment*	*Elements*
Contempt of Court Act 1981	• Contempt of court (s 9)	S	4	1 month	Tape recording
	• Contempt of court (s 12)	S	4	1 month	Wilful misbehaviour, insult or interruption
Control of Pollution Act 1974	Loudspeaker in street 9pm–8am	S	5[5]	—	
CYPA 1933	Cruelty to children	E	5	6 months	
Dogs (Protection of Livestock) Act 1953	Dog worrying livestock	S	3	—	
Factories Act 1961	Dangerous machinery	E	5	—	
Firearms Act 1968	• Firearm (tresspassing in a building)	E[6]	5[7]	6 months	
	• Firearm (tresspasser on land)	S	4	3 months	
	• Shotgun (without certificate)	S	5[7]	6 months	
	• No firearm certificate	E	5[7]	6 months	
	• Uncovered air weapon	S	3	—	
	• Loaded shotgun or air weapon or a firearm and ammunition without lawful excuse	E	5	6 months	
Forgery and Counter-feiting Act 1981	Forgery (ss 1, 3, 4)	E	5	6 months	Making, using or using a copy of a false instrument
Highways Act 1980	Obstructing highway	S	3	—	Without lawful authority or excuse wilfully obstructing free passage
Indecent Displays (Control) Act 1981	Public displays of indecent matter	E	5	—	Public place or licensed premises

Act	*Offence*	*Mode of trial*[1]	*Max fine*[2]	*Max imprisonment*	*Elements*
Indecency with Children Act 1960	Indecency with children	E	5	6 months	
Licensing Act 1872	Drunkenness	S	1	—	
Litter Act 1983	Littering	S	3	—	
Misuse of Drugs Act 1971	• Possession with intent to supply	E	5 3	6 months 3 months	class A, B drugs class C drugs
	• Possession	E	5 3 2	6 months 3 months	class A drugs class B, C drugs class C drugs
OAPA 1861	• Common assault (s 42)	S	3	2 months	
	• Assault ABH (s 47)	E	5	6 months	
	• GBH/Wounding (s 20)	E	5	6 months	
	• GBH with intent (S 18)	I			Intent to do grievous bodily harm or resist lawful dentention
Protection of Animals Act 1911	Cruelty to animals	S	4	3 months	
PA 1964	Police obstruction	S	3	1 month	Execution of duty (even if mistaken) or person assisting
Prevention of Crime Act 1953	Offensive weapon	E	5	6 months	
Public Order Act 1986	• Riot	I			
	• Violent disorder	E	5	6 months	
	• Affray	E	5	6 months	
	• Fear or provocation of violence	S	5	6 months	
	• Harrassment, alarm or distress	S	3	—	
Refuse Disposal (Amenity) Act 1978	• Abandoning motor vehicle	S	4	3 months	Taken with intent to abandon
	• Abandoning property	S	4	3 months	

Act	*Offence*	*Mode of trial*[1]	*Max fine*[2]	*Max imprisonment*	*Elements*
Regulation of Railways Act 1889	Fare avoidance	S	3	3 months	
Sexual Offences Act 1956	• Indecent assault	E	5	6 months	
	• Rape	E	5	6 months	
Social Security Act 1975	NI contributions	S	3[8]	—	
TA 1968	• Taking conveyance (s 12)				
	• Burglary	E	5	6 months	Entry, trespass, intent
	• Going equipped	E	5	6 months	
	• Handling stolen goods	E	5	6 months	Receiving, retaining or disposing, knowing or believing to be stolen
	• Abstracting electricity (s 13)	E	5	6 months	
	• Obtaining by deception (s 15)	E	5	6 months	Property
	• Obtaining by deception (s 16)	E	5	6 months	Pecuniary advantage
	• Theft	S	5	6 months	Appropriation of goods belonging to another, dishonesty, intention to permanently deprive
TA 1978	• Making off without payment (s 3)	E	5	6 months	
	• Obtaining by deception (s 1)	E	5	6 months	Services
	• Obtaining by deception (s 2)	E	5	6 months	Remission of liability
	• Obtaining by deception (s 2)	E	5	6 months	Inducing creditor to wait for payment
	• Obtaining by deception (s 2)				Exemption from liability
Trades Descriptions Act 1968	False trade description	E	5	Not imprisonable on summary conviction	

Act	*Offence*	*Mode of trial*[1]	*Max fine*[2]	*Max imprisonment*	*Elements*
Vagrancy Act 1824	• Indecent exposure • Enclosed premises	S S	3 3	3 months[9] 3 months[9]	
Wireless and Telegraphy Act 1949	No television licence	S	3	—	

Notes to table

1. S = summary only offence;
   E = offence triable either way;
   I = indictable only offence.
2. Level on standard scale.
3. Summary only for sums under £5,000.
4. Or 3 times duty evaded, whichever is greater.
5. Plus £50 per day after conviction.
6. Summary only for air weapons.
7. Plus forfeiture.
8. Plus compensation and arrears.
9. May be committed for sentence as an incorrigible rogue.

8 Costs and legal aid

The costs to be considered in any case in the magistrates' court are those of the prosecution, the defence and the court costs. Prosecution costs are those associated with the bringing of the case to court only and not the cost of the police investigation.

Defence costs are met from the legal aid fund or privately. Legal aid is available in virtually every criminal case other than straightforward road traffic cases in the magistrates' court, with the administrators thereof determining the appropriate contribution of the defendant. Legal aid costs other than the defendant's contribution are not included in costs orders. Defence barristers should bear in mind that they should apply for a certificate for counsel in appropriate cases, ie any indictable offence where the court is of the opinion that, because of circumstances which make the case unusually grave or difficult, representation by solicitor and counsel would be desirable (CJA 1982 s 30(2)) so that their fee is covered by the legal aid fund.

Statutes relevant to this chapter are the Costs in Criminal Cases Act 1973, the Prosecution of Offences Act 1985, and the Legal Aid Acts 1974 and 1988.

8.1 Costs

The POA 1985 ss 16–21 covers general rules as to costs in the magistrates' courts, and the various costs orders which can be made.

8.1.1 Costs against an opposing party

Section 19 of the POA 1985 provided that the Lord Chancellor should make provisions empowering the court to make an order for costs in favour of one party against the other where the court is satisfied that one party has, by an improper or unnecessary act or omission, incurred costs to the other party, which delegated powers are now in force. An order for costs in such a situation may be used to order the prosecution to pay a defendant's costs after proceedings, if such an act or omission has occurred, or if additional costs are incurred by any party due to any such act or omission by the other party. The court may then make provision for account to be taken of these additional costs when any order is made for the costs of the proceedings later.

Section 19 also provides for the payment out of central funds of witness expenses, interpreters expenses and the compensation of medical practitioners for their expenses in preparation of some reports although these were amended by the CJA 1988.

8.1.2 Defendant's costs from central funds

A defendants costs order, ie an order enforcing the payment of the costs of the defence, can be made where:

- any information charging any person with any offence is not proceeded with; or
- a magistrates' court inquiring into an indictable offence determines not to commit the defendant for trial; or
- a magistrates' court dealing summarily with an offence dismisses the information.

This order provides that the defendant be awarded his costs out of central funds, ie government or taxpayers money, and may also be made by the Crown Court after appeal from the magistrates' court if the appeal is successful. Legal aid costs are not included.

The order will be for an amount reasonably sufficient to compensate the defendant for any expense incurred in the proceedings unless the court considers that there are circumstances which make it inappropriate to award the full amount. In this case the order must specify the amount to be awarded which the court has assessed as just and reasonable (POA 1985 s 17). Then the amount will be specified and agreed by the defendant or will be determined in accordance with the Lord Chancellor's Regulations.

8.1.3 Prosecution costs from central funds

The prosecution may be awarded costs out of central funds in any proceedings in respect of an indictable offence (and in any proceedings before the Divisional Court or House of Lords in respect of a summary offence) such sum as the court considers reasonably sufficient to compensate them for any expenses properly incurred in the proceedings. However, such order can not be made in favour of any public authority including the CPS or a person acting on behalf thereof, or a person acting in his capacity as an official appointed by a public authority.

As for defence costs the court may consider that there are circumstances which make it inappropriate that the prosecution recover the full amount and assess a specified amount which, in its opinion, is just and reasonable. Equally, the amount will be specified and agreed by the prosecutor or be determined in accordance with the Lord Chancellor's Regulations. If the case has been taken over by the CPS an order for costs up to the intervention thereof in favour of the first prosecutor can be made.

8.1.4 Costs against the defendant

Costs against the defendant in favour of the prosecution may be awarded where he is convicted of any offence before the magistrates' court. The sum to be paid will then be such costs as the court considers just and reasonable subject to certain provisions:

- that if the court orders payment of a fine, penalty, forfeiture or compensation and the sum thereof is less than £5, then no order for costs shall be made unless there are particular circumstances whereby the court considers it right to do so;
- that any person under 17 shall not pay a sum in costs in excess of any fine imposed on him.

Note that the sum of costs will be determined after any other financial penalty has been set, and these and the defendants means will be taken into account when setting a just and reasonable sum.

8.2 Legal aid

Prior to the Legal Aid Act 1988, the legal aid fund established by statute was administered by The Law Society to help those in need with funds for legal representation. The fund is now administered by a separate Legal Aid Council and is available for the defendant in most criminal proceedings, but is not generally granted for road traffic offences and minor offences such as highway obstruction and not for the prosecution of criminal matters.

Some assistance is available under the scheme at police stations (PACEA 1984 s 58) or through the Green Form Scheme but this is limited to a total cost of £50 (or £90 for arrestable offences) whether provided by the Duty Solicitor or any other, though in some circumstances enhanced payments are made to the solicitor. Advice at police stations, unlike any other assistance, is free and not means tested. In the magistrates' court the Green Form Scheme provides mostly for assistance with domestic proceedings and is available by application to the solicitor consulted but can on occasion be extended.

Legal aid in criminal proceedings is available on the statutory criterion (LAA 1974 s 29) as to whether or not 'it is desirable to grant legal aid in the interests of justice where it appears that the person's means are such that he requires assistance in meeting the costs that he may incur', the benefit of any doubt being given to the applicant.

The criteria a court will usually use in individual cases were laid out by the 1966 Report of the Departmental Committee on Legal Aid in Criminal Proceedings chaired by Lord Widgery, and are commonly referred to as the Widgery Criteria. They suggest that legal aid will be granted if:

- the charge is murder;
- he defendant is in custody and likely to remain there on remand;
- a custodial sentence is likely (immediate or suspended);
- the defendant may lose his livelihood, or his reputation will be seriously damaged;
- a substantial question of law is raised;
- the defendant is disadvantaged in following the proceedings and stating his case, eg by a poor command of English or mental illness, or any other mental or physical condition;
- the defendant's case requires the pursuit of witnesses and interviewing thereof, or the assistance of an expert in cross examination of prosecution witnesses; or
- legal assistance is desirable in the interests of someone other than the defendant, eg in many sexual cases unless the defendant's means justify refusal.

8.2.1 Application for legal aid

Application for legal aid at court is commenced by the defendant completing the application form available from the court office or police stations. This can then be submitted to the court prior to the hearing by the solicitor but if this has not been done then, at a suitable time, the defendant or his representative should ask the court to indicate whether the case is suitable for legal aid subject to means. Where the defendant is unrepresented the justices' clerk should assist.

Grant or refusal of legal aid may be from the court, a justice, or the justices' clerk. If legal aid is refused, the first recourse would be to write to the justices' clerk to ask for a review including such additional details as support the application, which review will usually be granted.

Alternatively, a further application can be made in court, but the court will not often entertain such application unless there has been some significant change in circumstances and it is not a remand hearing. Where the offence is indictable only or triable either way, review by the Area Legal Aid Committee can be requested where refusal was on the grounds that it was not necessary in the interests of justice, such request to be made within 14 days of refusal and no less than 21 days before trial or committal.

The grant of legal aid will be accompanied by the drawing up of a certificate to that effect by the court clerk. A copy is sent to the defendant and to the solicitor who uses it to claim his costs in due course. The defendant will normally be able to appoint his own choice of solicitor but if there are a number of defendants the court may assign a single solicitor provided that there is no conflict of interests or opposition from any defendant in which case the parties should come to an agreement as to representation as far as possible.

8.2.2 Appeals

On appeal to the Crown Court, legal aid is available to the defendant and, on occasion, to the prosecutor as respondent. Advice on appeal is covered by the original legal aid order but for the appeal itself, application must be made either to the magistrates' court or to the Crown Court. However, legal aid for appeal to the High Court is obtained by application to the Area Committee of the Legal Aid Board.

9 Appeals

9.1 To the Crown Court

Only the defendant may appeal to the Crown Court. Furthermore, by MCA 1980 s 180:

- if he has pleaded guilty, he may only appeal against sentence unless the plea taken was equivocal. In this instance, affidavits may be asked for from the justices or their clerk. The Crown Court will then be the final arbiter on this issue. If it finds that the plea was equivocal the case will be remitted for a not guilty hearing;
- where a plea of not guilty was entered, appeal against sentence and/or conviction can be made to the Crown Court.

9.1.1 Procedure

Notice of appeal should be given within 21 days to the other party to the appeal and the clerk to the justices. Such notice need not state the grounds of appeal unless the statute is one listed in Pt III of Sched 3 to the Crown Court Rules 1982 (eg licensing) but must state whether the appeal is against sentence or conviction or both. Note that Part I of the same schedule lists Acts, such as the Firearms Act 1968, which make special provisions concerning procedure on appeal.

The appeal form will often be available at the magistrates' court. It is completed in triplicate and often a general ground of appeal will be given, eg that a sentence 'was in all the circumstances too severe' or that a conviction was 'against the weight of the evidence'.

Notice of the appeal must be given to the prosecution and they will usually require 24 hours notice of any hearing so that a prosecution representative can be present including at any bail application, etc.

Bail pending the appeal hearing can be asked for from the magistrates or, if this is not practicable or if bail is refused, by applying direct to the Crown Court. Notice of such application is still required but may, in exceptional circumstances, be waived by the prosecution.

An extension of time for lodging notice may be obtained by application in writing to the clerk to the Crown Court specifying the reasons for the application.

The course of the appeal will be a rehearing of the whole case including any additional evidence but the charge may not be amended and a conviction for an alternative offence may not be substituted. Whether the appeal is against conviction or sentence, any penalty which the magistrates' court could have imposed can be substituted and, therefore, a sentence can be increased as well as reduced which fact should be brought to the attention of the defendant.

Abandonment of the appeal is by notice in writing not less than three working days before the date fixed for the hearing. If the defendant is on bail pending the appeal (qv) he must surrender himself to the convicting court which may then proceed to enforce the sentence. An order for the costs of the abandonment may be made by the justices on the application of the other party.

9.2 To the High Court

9.2.1 Case stated

Any person who was a party to the proceedings before the magistrates' court or who is aggrieved by the conviction, order, determination or other proceedings of the court has the authority to question the decision on the grounds that it is wrong in law, or in excess of jurisdiction by applying for the case to be stated. Application is to the magistrates' court to state a case for the opinion of the High Court on the question and must be made within 21 days after the day on which the decision was given. The application is made in writing to the clerk to the justices and must identify the question or questions of law involved. The form is often available at the court and a specimen is reproduced in 'Stones Justices Manual'. This time limit can not be extended.

Amendment may be allowed where there is good reason. A recognisance, with or without a surety, may be required and the right of appeal to the Crown Court is lost unless the application relates to conviction only when an appeal to the Crown Court against sentence can still be made. Should the magistrates refuse to state a case there is a right of appeal against that refusal by application to the High Court for an order of *mandamus* requiring them to do so.

Grounds for application to the High Court are where a decision is wrong in law, where a bench come to a decision to which no reasonable bench could come (but not where this would reverse an acquittal in criminal proceedings which should be the result of judicial review), and indefensible decisions as to legal conclusions. In addition, application can be made on the grounds of 'excess of jurisdiction', eg passing of a sentence more severe than the law allows.

Alternatively to the above at paras 9.1 or 9.2, s 142 of the MCA 1980 gives the magistrates power to reopen a case within 28 days of their decision if there has been a procedural flaw or new evidence. However, s 42 cannot be used if there has already been an appeal in the Crown Court or High Court, or where the defendant is simply aggrieved without being able to show a procedural flaw or new evidence.

9.2.2 Judicial review

Judicial review of cases is a review by the High Court of proceedings and decisions of inferior courts and enables challenge of any act or omission of a magistrates' court as injudicious, or increasingly as 'contrary to natural justice', eg where there is a lack of jurisdiction or where there has been a denial of natural justice such as when the defendant is given no proper time to prepare his case.

Applications for prerogative order of prohibition, *mandamus* or *certiorari* may only be made by leave of the High Court which may be sought *ex parte* and supported by statement and affidavit. They should be made promptly and in any event within three months, and must be supported by statements supporting the application and specifying the relief sought and grounds thereof. Prohibitions may be absolute, temporary, or limited and restrain the magistrates' court from exceeding its jurisdiction or acting contrary to natural justice.

Mandamus is an order requiring an act to be done, eg requiring the magistrates' court to state a case or to hear a case remitted by the Crown Court following an equivocal plea.

Certiorari is an order commanding the magistrates' court to certify some matter of a judicial character and has the effect of removing proceedings from the magistrates' court to the High Court, ensuring that any matter is dealt with as appropriate, eg quashed.

Notice of the application must be made prior to the application and copies lodged with the Crown Office. Statements may be amended as to grounds, relief sought, or otherwise with the relief of the court. Any person with a sufficient interest in the matter may make an application for judicial review and that interest may be direct or general. Further rules relating to the content and hearing of applications are contained in RSC 1965 Ord 53.

Bail pending appeal (see Chapter 4) may be granted by the magistrates' court, the Crown Court or by the High Court.

9.3 Criminal Appeal Act 1995

Section 26 amends s 142 of the MCA 1980 and enables a magistrates' court to rehear a trial before a different bench, whether the defendant pleaded guilty or not, where it would be in the interests of justice to do so. This widens the magistrates' existing power by removing the 28 day time limit for reconsidering cases and thus makes a valuable contribution to the improvement in availability of appeals as it reduces the necessity to use other areas of appeal including judicial review.

10 Road traffic offences

Road traffic offences are often listed together in the magistrates' court, defendants having been informed by summons of the proceedings in the majority of cases. However, the most serious cases such as excess alcohol, driving whilst unfit and related offences, driving whilst disqualified or reckless driving are often the subject of a charge. Few offences are triable either way, and only causing death by dangerous driving is indictable only.

There is no special procedure in road traffic offences but certain rules have more common application particularly relating to:

- service of summons;
- proof in absence;
- warrants.

For this chapter, attention is given principally to offences brought to court by a summons being issued. At court the case is first called by the usher or other court staff. The defendant may appear but if he does not then the clerk will indicate whether service of the summons or adjournment notice has been effective.

10.1 Defendant not present

If the summons or other notice has not been served (by post) then on the first occasion the matter will be adjourned for further attempts, or personal service of the notice or summons, ie service by a police officer. If service of a summons can not be effected then the matter may be adjourned *sine die* so that at some future time the case can be resurrected or a warrant on information may be issued, if the information is put in writing and substantiated on oath and the offence is indictable or imprisonable. If service of a summons has been effected, the case will be listed for the entry of a guilty plea or to go over to a trial date for which witnesses, if required, will be warned and an adjournment notice to that effect will be sent to the defendant.

Pleas in many such traffic cases may be entered by post. If a guilty plea has been entered, the clerk will give the facts of the case and read any mitigation in the letter of the defendant. Then, if all documentation (licence or DVLC printout) is in order, the matter may be dealt with straightaway, but in a proportion of cases, eg if disqualification is being considered, the presence of the defendant will be required for sentencing.

If the defendant does not appear at the hearing, or has not replied to the summons or notice, and service is proved then the case can be proved in his absence, the prosecution evidence being called as if the defendant were present. Note that the defendant can also be found not guilty but, it would appear, not acquitted in his absence (*DPP v Gokceli* (1988) *The Times*, 10 October). It is usual in such circumstances to prove only the substantive offences, eg driving without insurance, and adjourn *sine die* any related offence, eg failing to produce insurance. In the event of a guilty finding then a warrant usually backed for bail can be issued if the offence is imprisonable or disqualification is being considered.

If the defendant is present then the matter proceeds as for any summary matter (or either way or indictable matter) for trial (or guilty plea or committal). At a hearing, attention will require to be paid to the usual rules of evidence and proof in criminal cases, but particular thought might be required in some cases on such disparate matters as:

- statute including EEC and tachograph regulations;
- excise duties;
- plating and testing of vehicles;
- vehicles adapted for special use; or
- operators' licences which unfortunately can not be considered in detail in this book.

In addition, evidence might be required by way of documents such as the memorandum of disqualification (from a previous offence), the statutory declaration of driver required from a vehicle owner, the police form HORT/2 to show that documents have not been produced at a police station or the printout from DVLC giving details of the defendant's driving licence, or lack thereof if his licence is not at court. For drink driving cases the readout from the evidential breath machine, or other analysis, should be available as well as any police documentation or medical evidence, etc. Medical evidence will be particularly persuasive in cases where the charge is driving whilst unfit rather than excess alcohol.

After a guilty plea or hearing, mitigation can be heard. If 'mitigating circumstances' or 'special reasons' are being put then evidence should be heard on these matters and magistrates are required to assess whether, on the balance of probabilities, these are sufficient for the relief of liability to the penalty (Wilkinson, Chapter 8).

10.2 Sentencing, penalty points and disqualification

In sentencing magistrates may, in addition to any fine or other penalty, be required to endorse the defendant's licence or disqualify him from driving depending on the offence proved. His presence is required for disqualification, and his licence or a printout from DVLC is needed for endorsements. Details of the sentencing limits for individual offences is given in the table on specific offences.

10.2.1 Endorsement

Following the Traffic Act 1981, endorsement is by way of penalty points, the points for each offence being specified either at a set value, or a value at the discretion of the magistrates within a certain range, by statute. This latter provision enables magistrates to endorse according to the severity of the incident in, for example, cases of careless driving, failing to stop after an accident, failing to give particulars after an accident, or using a motor vehicle with no insurance.

If two endorsable offences were committed at the same time, each is endorsed separately but the total of penalty points is entered as the highest of those for a single offence. If there are special reasons (see below) then magistrates may decide not to endorse for an offence where endorsement is 'obligatory'. An example might be where a driver gave his name and his company's address while driving a company vehicle instead of his own name and address as required. Endorsements are removed from a licence after a period of four to 10 years which depends on the offence in question.

10.2.2 Disqualification

Disqualification by totting up

Under the 'totting up' provisions of the Traffic Act 1981, penalty points from the instant offence are added to any still on the defendants record (points are removed for the purposes of totting up after three years of any disqualification). Magistrates are required to disqualify the defendant from driving for six months or more if the total exceeds 12 points unless there are mitigating circumstances for not disqualifying (or for disqualifying for a lesser period).

Mitigating circumstances are distinct from special reasons and include matters such as exceptional hardship (the loss of a job, for example, as a driver may be exceptional hardship but this is a matter of fact and degree in individual cases). The triviality of an offence, eg carefully passing through a red light which was stuck is not a mitigating circumstance but this or other matters may be put as a special reason for not endorsing so that the total for disqualification is not exceeded. A matter may not be put twice as a mitigating circumstance and for this reason the grounds for not disqualifying must be stated and entered in the register as fully as possible.

Disqualification for individual offences

Disqualification may be obligatory or discretionary. If obligatory for an offence then the minimum period will be 12 months or in some cases longer, eg second offences of drink driving within 10 years where the minimum is three years. Drink driving is the most common offence in this category, charged either as driving whilst unfit or driving with excess blood alcohol, ie a level exceeding 80 milligrammes per 100 millilitres of blood (107 mg per 100 ml urine or 35 microgrammes alcohol in 100 ml of breath).

In cases of obligatory disqualification, the only grounds for non disqualification are so called 'special reasons' which have been described variously by the King's Bench Division of Northern Ireland and the Court of Appeal (*R v Crossen* [1939] 1 NI 106 approved in *Whittall v Kirby* [1946] 2 All ER 552, *R v Wickens* [1958] 42 Cr App R 236).

The Court of Appeal laid down four criteria; that a special reason must:

- be a mitigating or extenuating circumstance;
- not amount in law to a defence to the charge;
- be directly connected with the commission of the offence; and
- be one which the court ought properly to take into consideration when imposing sentence.

Circumstances peculiar to the offender as distinguished from the offence are not, therefore, special reasons. It might be considered that the minor nature of an offence might fulfil the criteria but it is generally held that this fact alone is not a special reason (*Nicholson v Brown* [1974] RTR

177, *Marks v West Midlands Police* [1981] RTR 471). Unintentional commission, or commission after being misled (eg by a spiked drink) on the other hand is capable of amounting to a special reason as is a true emergency.

Discretionary disqualification may arise for most endorsable offences and may be applied in serious cases although the period is often short. In speeding, eg periods of 21–28 days are occasionally applied if the limit is exceeded by more than 30 miles per hour. In addition, it is possible to disqualify a person committing an endorsable offence who appears infirm or ill until they take and pass a driving test, and to disqualify or endorse anyone without a licence; DVLC being informed and keeping a note thereof.

Common road traffic offences

Offence[1]	*Licence endorsement*[2]	*Penalty points*[3]	*Offence code*	*Max fine*	*Max imprisonment*
Accident					
Failing to report	OE	8–10	AC 20	5	
Failing to stop	OE	8–10	AC 10	5	
Alcohol					
Refusing roadside breath test	OE	4	DR 10	3	
Failing to provide a specimen for analysis:					
• while in charge	OE	10	DR 60	4	3 months
• while driving	OD	4	DR 30	5	6 months
Driving whilst unfit (drink or drugs)	OD	4	DR 30	5	6 months
Drunk in charge of motor vehicle	OE	10	DR 50	4	3 months
Excess when in charge of vehicle	OE	10	DR 40	4	3 months
Excess when driving	OD	4	DR 10	5	6 months
Bicycle					
Defective brakes				3	

Offence[1]	*Licence endorsement*[2]	*Penalty points*[3]	*Offence code*	*Max fine*	*Max imprisonment*
Riding: • recklessly • without consideration • whilst unfit (drink)				 3 1 3	
Driving					
Careless	OE	2–5	CD 10	4	
Causing death by reckless driving	Crown Court only				
Recklessly	OE	3–11	DD 30	5	6 months
Without consideration	OE	3–9	CD 20	4	
Without due care	OD	3–9	CD 10	4	
Whilst disqualified: • by a court • by age	 OE OE	 6 2	 BA 10 BA 20	 5 5	 6 months
Without driving licence	OE	2	LC 10	3	
Uninsured	OE	6–8	IN 10	4	
Without L-plates	OE	2	PL 10	3	
Drugs – *see alcohol*					
Motor cyclist					
No helmet				1	
Unlawful pillion passenger	OE	3			
Pedestrian crossing					
Failing to stop	OE	3	PC 20	3	
Overtaking	OE	3	PC 30	3	
Stopping	OE	3	PC 30	3	
Seat belt					
Failing to wear				1	

Offence[1]	*Licence endorsement*[2]	*Penalty points*[3]	*Offence code*	*Max fine*	*Max imprisonment*
Speeding[3]					
Exceeding limit for road	OE	3–6	SP 30	3	
Exceeding limit for goods vehicle	OE	3–6	SP 10	3	
Exceeding limit for type of vehicle	OE	3–6	SP 20	3	
Exceeding limit on motorway	OE	3–6	SP 50	4	
Traffic directions					
Red traffic signal	OE	3–6	TS 10	3	
Constable or warden	OE	3–6	TS 40	3	
No entry	OE	3–6	TS 30	3	
Vehicle					
Defective brakes	OE	3	CU 10	4 (5 if goods vehicle or PSV)	
Without MOT certificate				3 (4 if goods vehicle)	
Defective tyres	OE	3	CU 30	4 (5 if goods vehicle)	
Vehicle excise licence					
Failing to display				1	
Using or keeping vehicle without				3 (or 5 times duty evaded plus back duty)	
Fraudulent use				5	

Notes to table

1 For notes on specific offences refer to Hannibal and Hardy, *Road Traffic Law*, 2nd edn, Cavendish, 1996.

2 OE = obligatory endorsement; OD = obligatory disqualification.

3 If a fixed penalty notice is issued the penalty points will be 3.

11 Problems in criminal proceedings

11.1 Joint defendants/severance

It is generally the rule that it is in the best interest of justice for joint defendants to be tried together for any offence. Nonetheless, an application to sever may be made but it will only be granted where there are overwhelming grounds for court trial; it is usual for all defendants jointly charged to be committed. Where one defendant elects Crown Court trial it has been more usual than not for all defendants jointly charged to be committed. However, *R v Brentwood JJ ex p Nicholls* and *R v Ipswich JJ ex p Callaghan* make it clear that such a decision must *not* be routinely taken.

A joint charge against a juvenile and an adult must be heard by a magistrates' court rather than a juvenile court (MCA 1980 s 29). However, where the adult pleads guilty and the juvenile not guilty the court has the power to remit to a juvenile court and may also remit when it is sitting as examining justices against the adult.

11.2 Multiple offences, tying up – committing or remitting

Where a defendant is charged with more than one offence he has the right to be tried separately for each but can opt for the matters to be tried together, and this is generally to be preferred. Problems can be encountered on those occasions when a defendant has a number of matters outstanding against him in a number of courts. If one of these is in the Crown Court, or is committed to the Crown Court, then by election the defendant can enable the matters to be brought together. However, if a guilty plea has been entered in the magistrates' court the justices' may commit for sentence (MCA 1980 s 38) or may prefer to defer sentence. Where all outstanding matters are in the magistrates' court then it may be possible to have them all remitted to a single court for sentence (MCA 1980 s 39).

11.3 Mode of trial

The prosecution opens the determination as to mode of trial and the main factor which affects this submission is the nature and seriousness of the offence, eg in assault the extent of any injuries and whether or not a weapon was used, whether a burglary was in domestic or industrial premises. Although the prosecution submission is persuasive the defence may make representations and a particular bench may have its own prejudices as to the seriousness of any offence. Additional factors to be taken into account by the defendant when considering a preferred mode of trial are that a summary trial will prove faster and cheaper, which fact will be reflected in any order for costs. In addition, the sentencing powers of magistrates are limited and it is generally considered that sentences passed are less than will be given in the Crown Court (although this is by no means certain). The disadvantage of summary trial is that it is considered that chances of conviction are higher, magistrates being thought of as case hardened, prosecution minded or simply less gullible.

11.4 Guilty plea – disputed facts

When the defendant wishes to plead guilty but there is a dispute as to the facts, eg amount stolen, nature of an assault or the extent of participation in a crime, then the justices should determine the facts upon which they will sentence by a 'Newton' style hearing. This will proceed by the hearing of evidence on both sides and the justices coming to their own conclusion (*R v Newton* (1983) 77 Cr App R 13).

11.5 Defendant failing to appear

Should the defendant fail to appear there are a number of options depending on the circumstances. The defendant can plead guilty by post to any summary only offence not punishable by more than three months imprisonment. This so called 'Magistrates' Courts Act Procedure' following MCA 1980 s 12 requires the prosecution to prove service of the summons together with a statement of the facts intended to put before the court. The clerk will read this statement and any mitigation put forward in writing. If necessary, the case can be adjourned and the defendant requested to attend for sentence or to clarify an equivocal plea.

If the court is satisfied that the defendant had sufficient notice of the hearing then it can proceed in his absence with a summary only offence or with summary trial of an either way offence provided that he was present or represented when the mode of trial was determined (MCA 1980 s 11), but the court may not pass any sentence of imprisonment, detention or disqualification. When trying a case in the defendant's absence, the court will still receive formal evidence on oath or by way of served statements. If convicted in his absence, the defendant may apply within 28 days to have the case heard under the provisions of MCA 1980 s 142. Alternatively, if he has known nothing of the offence or the proceedings, he can make a statutory declaration to that effect and apply to have the case reopened at any time (MCA 1980 s 14).

If the court requires the defendant to be present then it may issue a warrant or, if satisfied that there is a *bona fide* reason for non attendance, such as illness, simply enlarge bail until a suitable date. Warrants can be issued either through the powers of the Bail Act 1976 or MCA 1980. The Bail Act 1976 s 7 allows the issue of a warrant for the arrest of any person who fails to surrender to bail at the appropriate time, and on subsequent appearance this may be the subject of an additional charge of breach of the BA. The Magistrates' Courts Act 1980 s 1 empowers a justice to issue a warrant to bring any person before the magistrates' court but, before a warrant is issued, the information must be in writing and substantiated on oath. A warrant can not be issued under this section unless it relates to an indictable offence or an offence punishable by imprisonment or the persons' address is not sufficiently established for a summons to be served. If the defendant does not attend on a date fixed for a trial of any information then a warrant can be issued by virtue of MCA s 13 if the court decides not to proceed in his absence. Any warrant issued by the magistrates may be endorsed for bail as the court deems appropriate.

11.6 Prosecutor failing to appear

Should the prosecutor fail to appear the court may dismiss the information for want of prosecution or if evidence has already been heard proceed in his absence or adjourn the hearing.

11.7 Witness failing to appear

Where a witness fails to appear then either party may, in the first instance, apply for the case to be adjourned. However, where it is necessary, a witness summons may be issued (MCA 1980 s 97).

11.8 Amendments

Magistrates' Courts Act 1980 s 123 provides that amendments can be made to an information even if that information relates to a summary offence and is made outside the six month time limit. Amendments can be made at any time before the final disposal of the case. If the amendment is such that the defendant has been misled the court may, on application, adjourn the hearing. Therefore, if in the course of a trial an error comes to light, an application can be made to remedy the defect but it will be a question of fact and degree in each particular case whether the defect is so fundamental that the information ought to be dismissed.

11.9 Defendant unfit to plead

In cases where a defendant is unable or refuses to enter a plea there is no power for the magistrates to determine the question of his fitness to plead. If the charge is indictable only, they should proceed as examining justices to determine whether there is sufficient evidence on which to commit for trial. Where the offence is triable either way, they may decline jurisdiction and proceed as above. If they accept jurisdiction and the defendant is clearly not capable of making a decision as to mode of trial, they have the power, with the consent of his representative to make a hospital order under MHA 1983 s 37(3). The power to make a hospital order also exists if the defendant elects jury trial or for summary offences punishable with imprisonment but not for other summary offences where the case must proceed to trial.

11.10 Equivocal pleas

Where the defendant pleads guilty, either in person or by letter, and in the course of the proceedings puts forward facts or an explanation which discloses a defence to the charge then the court may enter a plea of not guilty on his behalf at any time before sentence.

12 Provisions for juveniles

Juvenile offenders in the law are those between the ages of 10 and attaining 18: Criminal Justice Act (CJA) 1991 s 68, given the rule that anyone under the age of 10 is not capable of committing any offence and for offenders between the ages of 10 and 14 there is a rebuttable presumption that they do not have the capacity to do so. (Certain offences may also be impossible by statute, for example, a child under 14 is incapable of rape.) Special sentencing provisions exist for offenders aged 18–20 and for this purpose only, these offenders, although once 18 technically adult, must be distinguished from those aged 21 and over.

Prior to court proceedings, the case will have been considered by a juvenile bureau (qv) to consider matters of public policy as to whether prosecution is appropriate. This chapter deals with the events thereafter and provisions for dealing with juveniles in the magistrates' court.

12.1 The youth court

The court must be specifically convened as a youth court and strictly separated from adult courts. Ideally, proceedings are held in a separate building but if this is not possible then there must be at least one hour between the sitting of the adult court and youth court. The youth court is the former juvenile court, renamed by the CJA 1991. Any reference in primary or other sources to the juvenile court should, therefore, now be understood to mean the youth court.

A juvenile offender will not in the first instance be dealt with by the youth court if he is charged jointly with an adult or he is to be tried on indictment, ie in the Crown Court, but trial on indictment is available for juveniles only if the offence is one of homicide or he is charged jointly with an adult on an indictable offence, or the offender is over 14 and the offence is 'grave', ie an adult could be sentenced to a term of imprisonment exceeding 14 years. However, the matter may in certain circumstances be remitted to the court for sentence or trial.

The bench in a youth court will consist of magistrates, normally three, selected from a special panel comprising largely those magistrates with experience in working with children and also stipendiary magistrates, but a stipendiary magistrate may on occasion sit alone.

Both the parents of the defendant should attend but one of them or a guardian must usually do so. Except where the child or young person is legally represented, this parent or guardian is allowed to assist in the conduct of the defence including the cross examination of prosecution witnesses. The juvenile is referred to throughout by his christian name (or familiar name, nickname). Proceedings in a youth court are confidential with only court officials and those connected with the case present. In particular, solicitors and their clients have no right to be in court before their cases begin, and there may be a difficulty where their cases involve social workers or probation officers who seem to remain in court regardless of whether they are personally engaged in the case in progress. The press are allowed but can not disclose any information regarding the identity of the defendant, except where an application is made on behalf of the juvenile and it would avoid an injustice to him or, in circumstances where the juvenile is unlawfully at large, on application by the DPP.

12.2 Procedure

The distinct atmosphere of the youth court is emphasised by differences in terminology from those used in the adult magistrates' court and by a difference in practice and formalities.

The court having accepted the case, after determining mode of trial if necessary, the charge is read and the court has a duty to explain the charge in simple language before asking the defendant whether he pleads guilty or not guilty to the charge.

At this time the issue as to the child's age and capacity to commit a crime may also be considered. It should be borne in mind that the prosecution must prove that a child under 14 has the capacity to commit the offence (*doli incapax*) and adduce any relevant evidence notwithstanding its prejudicial value (*R v B*; *R v A* [1979] 1 WLR 1185). If the age of the child is not known then he may be deemed a certain age by the court for the purpose of the proceedings after asking such questions as appear relevant. If the child attains the age of 18 during the course of proceedings, he may not be further charged in that court thereafter but matters in progress may be completed. If he is 18 at plea, he must be sent to the adult magistrates: *Ex parte Taylor* (1992) 93 Cr App R 365. His right to elect Crown Court trial is determined by his age on the date on which the mode of trial is determined (*R v Lewes Juvenile Court ex parte T* (1984) *The Times* 28 July). As far as sentencing is concerned, if the juvenile reaches the age of 18 during the course of proceedings, the court may deal with the penalty as though the offender were still 17: CYPA 1963 s 29. It should be noted that technically the court does not 'sentence' but 'make an order on a finding of guilt' (nor do they 'convict' but instead 'record a finding of guilt'): CYPA 1993 s 59.

If the plea is one of not guilty, the court proceeds to hear the evidence of witnesses in support of the charge, each of whom may be cross examined by or on behalf of the juvenile. When giving evidence there is no oath in the youth court, but all witnesses, adults and children alike, promise before Almighty God to tell the whole truth and nothing but the truth: CYPA 1993 s 59.

Where the juvenile is not represented or assisted in his defence and he makes assertions instead of asking questions by way of cross examination, it is the duty of the court to put such questions as it thinks necessary to a witness and, in order to do so, the juvenile may be questioned to bring out or clear up any point arising.

If it appears to the court that a *prima facie* case has been made out then if the child or young person is not legally represented he must be told that he may give evidence or address the court and the evidence of any witnesses for him will then be heard.

If the juvenile is found guilty, whether after a guilty plea or a not guilty plea, he and his parent or guardian will be given an opportunity to make a statement before sentencing. In arriving at a sentence, the court must take into consideration such information as to the general conduct of the juvenile as may be necessary to enable it to deal with the case in his best interests. In particular, reference should be made to those factors mentioned in CYPA 1969 s 9 namely, the home surroundings, school record, health and character of the defendant. If such information is not available, the court will consider an adjournment to enable such enquiry as may be required to be made.

Written reports can be received and considered without being read aloud and, if it is necessary in the interests of the child, the parent or guardian may be required to withdraw from the court.

Copies of any report before the court should be made available to any parent or guardian of the child present at the hearing, the child himself (except when the court directs otherwise) and his legal representative. The child or his parent or guardian should be told the substance of any information the court considers material (to the manner in which the case should be dealt with) which relates to their character or conduct.

The parent or guardian should also be told the substance of any material which has reference to home surroundings or the health of the child, and if they then wish to adduce further evidence to the court relating to this information then the court should adjourn the proceedings to give them an opportunity to do so.

Before finally disposing of the case or remitting it to another court the child, his parent or guardian, or his legal representative should be informed of the proposed manner of dealing with the case to allow them to make representations (unless the court considers it undesirable to so inform the juvenile himself).

On making any order the court shall explain the general nature and effect of the order to the child or young person unless it is an order requiring his parent or guardian to enter into a recognisance and it appears undesirable to so explain.

12.3 Adjournment, remand and bail

On adjournment of a case in the youth court then the issue of bail arises in the same way as in the adult court. Bail is a general right of the defendant and subject to the same conditions as described in Chapter 4 but bail may also be refused on the ground that it is necessary for the child's welfare.

If bail is granted then conditions may be attached, including sureties. If a parent is the suretor then it is possible for the surety to apply to any condition and not just to the surrender to custody as in the adult court. If bail is not granted then the possibilities are remand in care, remand in secure accommodation, or remand in a remand centre or prison. In such circumstances, the maximum period of remand is eight days, unless accident or illness intervenes.

Remand in secure accommodation or a remand centre is available only in certain circumstances. Secure accommodation orders can only be made if the court believes that the defendant is likely to abscond or likely to injure himself or others, and the offence is grave or an offence of violence. He may only be remanded in secure accommodation for up to 72 hours without reference to the youth court unless the criteria set out in the Child Care Act 1980 s 21A are fulfilled (Secure Accommodation [No 2] Regulations 1983 Reg 7).

12.4 Sentencing

Provisions for sentencing of juveniles are considered in Chapter 3. In adducing antecedents, juvenile cautions may be relevant but unless recent, of a similar nature, or against the same individual, they need not be mentioned, as although they are admissions of guilt they are not convictions. Note that some penalties can be imposed on the parents of the juvenile, including fines, and that parents can be bound over by the court. See para 3.4.4 above.

12.5 Juvenile checklist

- Age: relevance to culpability (*doli incapax*), sentence, etc
- Bail: previous record, nature of offence, unruliness
- Gravity of offence
- Parent in attendance
- Background including reports if appropriate, previous convictions/cautions
- Means, including casual work, eg Saturday jobs, newspaper rounds
- An offence for which an adult could be imprisoned for 14 years
- Binding over parents

13 Liquor licensing

Licensing is one of the few areas of commercial life impinging on the magistrates' court, and one where local considerations are of some importance. Legal aid is not available in licensing matters and costs of representation are borne by the applicant with a fee payable for the licence.

Magistrates have jurisdiction to consider matters within the area of the court relating to the grant and holding of licences to sell liquor, for restaurants, and for betting and gaming licences. In any area, applications are generally required to go to the relevant district licensing committee, although certain applications such as for a protection order can be heard by justices sitting as a magistrates' court.

The law relating to licensing of persons and premises for the sale of liquor is given principally by the Licensing Act 1964 amended by the Licensing Act 1988.

Applications are made to the district licensing committee which comprises five to 20 magistrates from that district. The committee is required to hold at least four transfer sessions a year and to hold an annual general licensing meeting. No magistrate may sit on the licensing committee if debarred on grounds of a direct interest in brewing or a related industry, or an undeclared interest by way of shares, etc, or an interest in the premises being considered.

Three magistrates form a quorum for the hearing of a licensing application which proceeds democratically, ie a majority of the bench must decide in favour of the application for it to succeed (abstention counting as a vote against).

Licensing applications may be for renewal, extension or transfer, of existing licenses or for new licences as well as occasional permissions such as those for school fetes, etc. Applications for renewal should be heard at the annual general meeting usually held in the first two weeks of February, whilst other applications may be heard at transfer sessions.

Applicants before a licensing committee may be unrepresented, represented by a solicitor or barrister or be represented by some other person such as a representative of his employer or an agent, whereas if magistrates are sitting as a court in petty sessions, a solicitor or barrister alone may act as representative.

13.1 Procedure

Prior to the hearing, notice of any application must be given to the local authority, the police, the court and the fire authority. Except for transfer or renewal of licenses, the notice must also be displayed on the premises in question and in a local newspaper prior to the hearing.

Procedure of licensing committees is unregulated but in practice procedures similar to those used for the hearing of a complaint in civil proceedings are followed, the applicant(s) speaking and calling evidence first followed by the police and then any other parties, usually objectors. All evidence is usually required to be on oath.

An outline of the application is given by the applicant's representative and evidence in support of the application is then called, with attention given to establishing suitability of the application and then the matters relevant to the statutory and discretionary grounds for grant or refusal of an application.

In any application the applicant should be called first and asked to state his name and address (if he is an employee he may be accompanied by a representative of his prospective employers). He should give evidence or be asked by his advocate to state that he has seen a list of disqualified persons and that these conditions do not apply to him. Persons disqualified (Licensing Act 1964 s 9) are:

- a sheriff's officer or an officer executing the legal process of any court;
- a person convicted, whether under the LA 1964 or otherwise, of forging a justices' licence or making use of such a forged licence knowing it to be forged;
- a person convicted of permitting to be a brothel premises for which at the time of conviction he held a justices' licence.

The applicant should then give information relevant to the application, the licence he wants and the premises. He should outline his knowledge of the statutory terms of the licence, particularly his knowledge of the licensing hours and persons who may not be served, as well as his relevant experience including attendance at training courses, and general knowledge of the licensing laws and offences. Particular attention should then be paid to matters peculiar to each licence outlined below and to local matters: need, problems with traffic or trouble spots.

Clear evidence must also be given as to how the premises are to be run and what staffing will be, storage facilities and other relevant factors. It is also helpful if the existing licence holder is in court to show his support for the application.

Objectors, usually led by a police officer, will then be asked to give their evidence. Objections from the police may include previous convictions, inexperience or language difficulties as well as other evidence to show unsuitability of the licensee as well as evidence as to unsuitability of the premises, excess of existing provision or other matters.

13.2 Permitted licensing hours (LA 1964 Pt III including ss 59, 60, 62, 67A, 68, 70, 74, amended by LA 1988 s 1)

The general rules of licensing hours applicable are tabulated below. Hours may, however, be modified by the licensing committee through various provisions such as general orders of exemption, special orders of exemption, occasional permissions, and extended hours orders, and they do not apply to occasional licences where the hours are those specified in the licence. These hours may also be subject to restriction orders or voluntary closure by the licensee.

General

Weekdays: 11 am to 11 pm

Sundays, Christmas Day, Good Friday: 12 noon to 10.30 pm

Off licences

As above but starting at 8 am on weekdays, and 10 am on Sundays.

Clubs

- Licensed (propietary); as for justices' licences.
- Registered clubs; general licensing hours, except Christmas Day where the hours must be no more than 6 and a half in total beginning no earlier than noon and ending no later than 10.30 pm, with a break including the hours 3–5 in the afternoon.

13.3 Persons not to be served

Persons under 18 may not be served alcohol, and may not consume liquor except in certain cases where they are served alcohol as an adjunct to food. Other persons who may not be served are constables in uniform and drunks.

13.4 Refusal of licence, appeal, provisional licences

Should any application for an on licence be refused, it remains open to the applicant to apply without further notice for a restaurant licence, a residential licence or a combined restaurant and residential licence, should this be suitable. An unsuccessful applicant or objector also has the right of appeal to the Crown Court. Applications for a provisional licence can be made for proposed premises on the basis of plans submitted to the licensing committee.

13.5 Types of licence

Liquor licence applications may be for one of any of the following: on licences, off licences, restaurant licences, residential licences, club licences, or occasional licences. Each presents its own set of rules and the grounds of refusal and the conditions relevant to each of these are presented below.

13.5.1 On licences

Points to be considered for an on licence application are:

- that the premises are structurally sound and adapted for the purpose especially in relation to storage, fire risks and toilet facilities;
- that the proposed licensee is a suitable person to hold a licence and is not disqualified from doing so, ie an officer executing the legal process of any court, a person convicted of forging a justices' licence or using such a licence knowing it to be forged, or a person convicted of permitting premises for which he held a justices' licence to be used as a brothel;
- that there is a local need; this is not a requirement of the Licensing Act but is now a widely accepted requirement;
- in reaching a decision, the court will often examine the applicant as to his experience and his knowledge of licensing laws (ie licensing hours, prohibition on sales, etc);
- that staffing, supervision and security is adequate.

Magistrates may attach conditions as to the type of liquor which can be sold, ie wine only; cider only; beer, wine and cider only; or beer and cider only.

13.5.2 Off licences

Requirements for an off licence are similar to those for an on licence but the application itself should specify the category of liquor intended to be sold, ie either any intoxicating liquor or beer, wine and cider only.

13.5.3 Restaurant and residential licences

In considering restaurant or residential licence applications, magistrates should be satisfied that:

- the premises are suitable structurally and otherwise for the purpose, ie the provision of a midday or evening meal, or the provision for reward of board and lodging, including breakfast and one of the main meals in the day;
- the applicant is over 18 and a fit and proper person;
- a large proportion of customers are not under 18 and unaccompanied by and paid for by a person over 18;
- liquor is not sold on a self service basis;
- the application has not arisen after forfeit within the last 12 months of an on licence;
- police and other authorities have been able to inspect the premises on request;
- there has been no bad conduct of the premises or breach of any licence conditions; and
- the meals provided are such that ancillary alcoholic beverages are appropriate.

Conditions which attach to restaurant licences are:

- that other non alcoholic beverages are provided; and
- that alcohol is provided only with meals.

However, other conditions may be specified by the committee.

13.5.4 Residential licences

For residential licences, the statutory conditions are that intoxicating liquor may only be supplied to residents or their *bona fide* guests being entertained at the residents' expense, to be consumed on the premises or with a meal supplied at the premises, and that unless there is a good reason paying guests should be provided with a sitting room where intoxicating liquor or substantial refreshment is not served.

13.6 Transfer and removal of licences

Applications to change a licence by transfer or removal are also heard by licensing justices. Transfer is the change from one person to another whereas removal refers to the change from one premises to another. Transfer applications can only be heard at licensing sessions and the committee must be satisfied that the proposed licensee is a fit and proper person relying heavily on police enquiries and whether they have any objections. Procedure is the same as for other applications although for transfer the only matter strictly at issue is the suitability of the intended licensee, ie that he is a 'fit and proper person'.

Transfer can only be effected in cases if:

- the licensee has died; then transfer can be to the new tenant, the occupier of the premises or the representative of the deceased;
- the licensee is incapable through illness; then transfer to his assignee, a new tenant or occupier can proceed;
- the licensee is bankrupt; the transfer can pass to the trustee, new tenant or occupier; and
- the licensee (or his representatives) is about to give up the premises to the new tenant or occupier.

If the outgoing occupant has wilfully neglected or omitted to apply for renewal then transfer of the licence can be effected to the new tenant or occupier, and if the owner or his agent has been granted a protection order (qv) then the licence can be transferred to this owner or his agent.

Application for removal of a licence is to the licensing committee of the area where the proposed premises are situated, and may include an application for transfer. The committee must be satisfied that there is no objection to the removal from any person they consider has a right to object, particularly the present licensee (if different from the applicant) or the owner of the present premises. The proposed premises must comply with the planning requirements outlined above but otherwise the committee may have no objection.

13.7 Protection orders

Protection orders are granted by magistrates in petty sessions and not by the licensing committee. They temporarily authorise someone other than the licensee to exercise the licensee's rights of selling at the premises, and are effective until the second licensing session after the date of the protection order. Notice must be given to the police prior to application and may only be granted if the justices are satisfied that the applicant is a person entitled to be granted a transfer at a licensing session. A second protection order can be granted in circumstances where a first applicant is not qualified for a transfer, or no longer intends to apply for transfer or is no longer able to carry on the business.

13.8 Application to alter premises

Application to alter licensed premises is required prior to the alteration, except if the alteration has been ordered by lawful authority. If the alteration increases drinking facilities in a part of the premises which is open to all or some residents, or if they conceal from observation any part of the premises used for drinking, or if they affect communication then application is required. Notice is only required to the clerk of the court with a plan of the proposed alterations but it is strongly advised that notices be sent to the police, local authority and fire authority.

13.9 Club licences, and other liquor licences

Clubs may be either licensed or registered and application for designation is by annual application to the licensing sessions. The licence is essentially a conditional on licence and permitted hours differ from those of public houses.

Other applications for liquor licensing relate to occasional licences, occasional permission, special and general orders of exemption (extensions) and various other certificates covering extended hours, eg a special hours certificate, extended hours order or a supper hour certificate. A full discussion of these applications is beyond the scope of this book.

Notices required to be sent in liquor licence applications

	On licences *Off licence* *Part IV licence*	*Transfer*	*Protection*
Clerk	Yes	Yes	Advised
Police	Yes	Yes	Yes
Licensee	N/A	Yes	Yes
Local authority	Yes	Yes	No
Fire authority	Yes	No	No
Newspaper	Yes	No	No
Premises	Yes	No	No
Deposition of plans	Yes*	No	No

* Except for on licence

14 Betting and gaming licences

14.1 Betting licences

Applications for a bookmaker's permit or a betting office licence are regulated principally by the Betting Gaming and Licensing Act 1963. They are heard by magistrates from the betting licence committee. This committee is comprised, in the same way as a liquor licensing committee, of at least five and no more than 15 magistrates appointed at the Annual General Meeting of local magistrates each October.

14.1.1 Procedure

Application involves the service of a number of statutory notices, including one upon HM Customs and Excise. Procedure at the hearing is as for liquor licences, the applicant giving evidence first then any objector. The applicant's suitability should be established as well as the suitability of the premises and the existing demand, if a new application is being made. Otherwise attention should be paid to the statutory and discretionary grounds for refusal of the licence in question.

14.1.2 Bookmaker's permit

Magistrates must refuse to grant or renew a bookmaker's permit if the applicant is under 21 years, or he is disqualified by reason of convictions for betting offences or other offences involving dishonesty, or if he has not been resident in Great Britain for the last six months. It must also refuse if the applicant has been refused a bookmaker's permit or betting agency permit during the last 12 months because the committee was not satisfied that he was a fit and proper person, or if he has had his bookmaker's permit cancelled during the last 12 months. The committee may also refuse if it is not satisfied that the applicant is a fit and proper person, or if it is satisfied that the grant or renewal would be for the benefit of a person who would be refused a permit.

14.1.3 Betting office licence

Discretionary grounds for refusing a betting office licence are that the committee must refuse if it is not satisfied that the applicant will hold a bookmaker's permit or betting agency permit when the licence comes into force (unless the applicant is the Tote Board), or if it is not satisfied that the premises are or will be enclosed, or that the betting office will have its own means of access to the street. The committee may refuse on the grounds that the premises are not suitable, or that it is inexpedient for the locality, or that the premises have not been properly conducted under the licence in force.

Cancellation of betting licences can be applied for by any person but such application must be refused if the committee is satisfied that the matters raised have been or ought to have been raised when the permit was originally granted.

Notices required for betting licence applications

	Bookmaker's permit	*Betting agency permit*	*Betting office licence*
Notices for grant of licence			
Clerk	✓	✓	✓
Police	✓	✓	✓
Local authority			✓
Press advertisement (copy to clerk)	✓	✓	✓
Notice on premises			✓
Notices for renewal of licence			
Clerk	✓	✓	✓
Police			
Local authority			
Press advertisement (copy to clerk)			
Notice on premises			

14.2 Gaming licences

Provisions relating to the grant of gaming licences are principally given by the Gaming Act 1968. Gaming licences are issued by application to the Betting Licensing Committee but, prior to the application, a certificate of consent must be obtained from the Gaming Board. Gaming licences include full licences or bingo club licences. A bingo club licence is simply a gaming licence restricting the type of gaming to bingo.

Application for a gaming licence may be made at any time using the prescribed procedure. At the hearing, procedure follows that for other licence applications; objectors may include the Gaming Board who have a right of appeal against decisions made. The licence may be refused if:

- the committee is not satisfied that a substantial demand already exists for the proposed gaming;
- the layout, character, condition or location of the premises are not satisfactory;
- the applicant is not a fit and proper person; or he is a front for other unfit or improper persons;
- the premises have not been made available for inspection;
- gaming duties have not been paid;
- the premises are not in a prescribed licensed club area;
- there is direct access to the premises from other private premises not in the licence; or
- if there are valid objections.

Compulsory restrictions banning dancing, music, live entertainment or, if appropriate, bingo must be included on each licence. Licences, if granted, last for 12 months and application for renewal must be lodged 2–5 months before the renewal date. Only the Gaming Board or a dissatisfied applicant can appeal, such appeal going to the Crown Court.

Other Gaming Act registrations in Pt II and Pt III of the Gaming Act effected by the Betting Licensing Committee include those for gaming machines as well as the registration of members' clubs for gaming.

14.2.1 Notices required for gaming licence applications

In applications for grant or renewal of a licence, notices should be sent to the clerk of the court, police, local authority, fire authority, Gaming Board and the customs and excise collector of duty. In addition, in applications for grant of a licence, a gaming board certificate, press advertisement and notice posted on the premises is required.

15 Matrimonial, domestic and child care proceedings

15.1 The family proceedings court

Various domestic proceedings can be brought in the magistrates' court and a full discussion is beyond the scope of this note, particularly with the expansion in the number of cases heard since the introduction of the Children Act 1989 (see Mitchels, *Child Care and Protection, Law and Practice*, 2nd edn, Cavendish 1996). Those which will be considered in outline here relate to orders for maintenance, orders for residence and contact relating to children and adoption. Individual matters may involve application for more than one such order. Wherever possible in such proceedings conciliation and agreement should be sought to simplify issues and reduce future conflict, and it is often said that a common sense approach is of benefit.

Cases must be heard by a family proceedings court, comprising justices from the family panel. This panel is appointed by the justices for an area by nomination or ballot from suitable and willing justices, those with the necessary qualities and if possible experience (including one or more with experience of adoption proceedings). These justices are then required to undertake basic training and instruction.

15.2 Procedure

Matrimonial or domestic matters are usually begun by issuing an application before a justice or justices' clerk, who may then issue a notice to the respondent to attend and answer. The application may be originating the particular litigation or be to vary earlier orders after a change of circumstances. In matters such as child care proceedings, an initiation of proceedings requires also the service of notices on a number of parties laid out as relevant in each section below.

In many cases, the first hearing will be before the court clerk, for directions. This will often be conducted in the presence of a court welfare officer and will aim at conciliation between the parties. At this stage, representations as to whether the case is appropriate for the magistrates' court may also be heard. If the case is complex or likely to run for more than three days, then a county court will usually be the preferred venue and the case may be transferred. The further aim of the directions hearing is to ensure that the administration of the case is in order. Usually, a hearing date will be fixed, time limits for filing of statements will be set and a court welfare report may be ordered, perhaps limited to the remaining contentious issues.

The procedure at hearing follows that in the county court and is laid out in the Magistrates Court Rules r 14. Oral evidence is preferred with the applicant opening and calling all evidence in support of the application and the respondent cross examining. If possible, an agreed chronology, paginated bundle and index should be available and it is advisable to prepare a skeleton argument for cases involving children. All cited authorities should be provided.

In opening, the background of the case should be put, eg date of marriage, birth of children, etc and a description of the remedy sought with outline grounds of the application. Evidence should then be called, beginning with the applicant, to give details such as incidents of violence, if relevant, and any recent events.

In cases where children are involved particular attention must also be given to the 'welfare checklist' and the 'welfare principle' set out in the Children Act 1989. Attention should be given to factors relating to provision for them including type and quality of housing, proximity to schools, facilities for supervision of the children at their place or residence or during contact.

The applicant then gives his evidence and is cross examined, before further evidence and witnesses are called to speak on his behalf. The respondent(s) or defendant may then give evidence and call further evidence, before an address by the applicant. Either party may then apply to further address the court, and the other party must not then be refused if he applies in turn. If the court then decides that the case may more conveniently be dealt with by the High Court, it should refuse to make any order (DPMCA 1978 s 27). Otherwise the magistrates will retire to reach a decision by agreement or majority verdict.

In giving their decision, the justices must also announce their reasons for the decision which will be recorded at the time. The case may proceed in the absence of the respondent if service has been proved and effected a reasonable time before the hearing (MCA 1980 s 55). If the applicant fails to appear, the complaint may be dismissed, or if evidence has been received on a previous occasion, the court may proceed in their absence (MCA 1980 s 56). Where a party is legally represented, he will be deemed not to be absent unless his presence is specifically required by enactment or recognisance. Appeal lies to the High Court in the case of most domestic proceedings.

15.3 Costs

Legal aid is available for most proceedings and advice can be sought through the Green Form scheme, then extended on application to the area legal aid committee to cover full representation in court. In considering such an application, the committee must be convinced that the case of the person applying is worthy of consideration and that representation is necessary for the case to be presented fairly. Where the matter is straightforward, for example, variation of an existing monetary order, the court will usually be able to extract all relevant information without representation and legal aid may not be granted.

The court may order the payment of the whole or part of the costs of a party to be paid by the other party (MCA 1980 s 64). As in other cases, an unsuccessful party is rarely awarded costs, and costs are not always awarded to a successful party particularly if agreement should have been reached.

15.4 Examples of common applications

15.4.1 Maintenance

The magistrates' court has the jurisdiction to consider applications under DPMCA 1978 ss 2, 6 and 7 and CA 1989 for payment of maintenance, periodical payments or lump sums to a spouse, former spouse or child of a family. In addition, application for an order in respect of a child may be made under the Child Support Act 1991.

Orders by virtue of the DPMCA 1978 s 2 may be made after application by a spouse on the grounds that the respondent has:

- failed to provide reasonable maintenance for the applicant;
- failed to provide or make proper contribution towards maintenance of any child of the family;
- behaved in such a way that the applicant cannot reasonably be expected to live with the respondent;
- has deserted the applicant.

Sections 6 and 7 are applications arising out of agreements or practice as to making of maintenance payments or other type of periodical payment for the benefit of a spouse or child of the family, whilst CA 1989 is appropriate in cases where a residence or contact order is made in respect of any child of the family.

In making any maintenance order, the court should consider first, the welfare of any child and then the income, earning capacity and other financial resources of each party, their financial needs, obligations and responsibilities, and the standard of living each enjoyed prior to the application. These details should be ascertained by the advocate prior to court to assist in the hearing and, where possible, a written statement of means set out in a schedule of means should be prepared on the lines of the example shown below, for a husband remarried after divorce from his first wife who is making an application for maintenance of a child from his first marriage. Where possible wage slips and bills should be presented.

Example schedule of means

John A Smith

Income	£ per week
Income (Net)	125.00
Wife's income (Net)	50.00
Total	175.00

Expenses	£ per week
Mortgage	60.00
Rent/rates	20.00
Gas	3.50
Electricity	4.00
Car HP	12.50
Car expenses and petrol (Mr Smith)	7.50
Car expenses (Mrs Smith)	6.50
TV licence	1.00
Total	115.00

A similar statement of means from the other party should be available and allows for the calculation of an appropriate maintenance figure. Where any figure appears excessive or unnecessary in the circumstances, eg a second car, the party should be cross examined on that point.

Secondary considerations are the age of each party, duration of the marriage, physical or mental disability, the contributions of each party to the family welfare and finally the conduct of each of the parties. If the application is for child maintenance then the financial needs of the child as well as the factors mentioned above should be considered. The court may order the payment to be made direct to the applicant or through the court. In the case of non payment the court may make an attachment of earnings order to ensure future payment, or commit a regular offender to prison for a period not exceeding six weeks.

At any time, it is open to either party to apply for an interim order or a variation of orders, eg if circumstances have changed.

15.4.2 Orders relating to residence and contact with children

In reaching a decision as to residence and/or contact, the welfare of the child is the first and paramount consideration. Having considered this, the court may make an order under CA 1989 for residence. Where an order for residence is made, it is usual to make at the same time an order for contact to the other party which will often be simply for 'reasonable contact' which is then agreed by the parties.

15.4.3 Personal protection orders and exclusion orders

Either party to a marriage may apply to the court for an order that the respondent shall not use or threaten violence against the applicant or a child of the family. Before making such an order, the court must be satisfied that the respondent has used or threatened violence and that the order is necessary for the protection of the applicant or child. A personal protection order under DPMCA 1978 s 16(2) can then be made. If the respondent has also used violence upon some other person or is in breach of an order under s 16(2) and the applicant or child is in physical danger or would be in danger if they entered the matrimonial home, the court may make an exclusion order: s 16(3) and s 16(4).

15.4.4 Adoption proceedings

Adoption applications proceed according to the Magistrates' Courts (Adoption) Rules 1984. Application may be made jointly only by a married couple, but may be made by one person provided he is over 21 years and is domiciled in the UK, Channel Islands or the Isle of Man.

Applications are heard *in camera* and, in dealing with an application, the court should have regard to the possibility of custodianship as an alternative.

No order can usually be made without the unconditional agreement of the child's actual parents or legal guardian. The agreement of the father of an illegitimate child is not necessary unless he is the legal guardian and agreement can be dispensed with if:

- the parent or guardian cannot be found;
- the child has been neglected, ill treated or abandoned;
- the parent is withholding agreement unreasonably; or
- the parent has failed, without reasonable cause, to discharge his parental duties.

Parental agreement is also not necessary if the child has been 'freed for adoption', an order made when adoption proceedings are not imminent but are contemplated for the future.

15.5 Child care proceedings

Child care proceedings in the magistrates' court relate principally to applications for care or supervision orders by the local authority. They include applications for emergency protection, care and supervision orders, as well as proceedings for variation and discharge of such orders.

Applications for care or supervision orders are usually brought by a local authority and, to support such an order, the court must be satisfied that there is a likelihood of significant harm. Possible grounds for such a finding are:

- if the development of the child is neglected;
- if another child in the same household is neglected;
- exposure to moral danger;
- if the child is beyond the parents' control;
- if the child is not receiving efficient full time education;
- if the child is guilty of an offence.

Other applications may then arise to vary or discharge the original order if there is a change of circumstances.

15.5.1 Procedure

Applicants proposing to bring proceedings send notice to the clerk of the court specifying the grounds and the names and addresses of those to whom copies have been sent. These persons will usually be:

- the infant (unless it is inappropriate);
- his parent or guardian;

- any grandparent;
- any foster parent;
- the local authority

and, if necessary, the child's probation officer or supervisor.

On receipt of the notice, the respondent(s) should then, within 14 days, inform the clerk as to whether he intends to oppose the application. Often, it may arise at this stage that there is a possible conflict of interest between child and parent. This may give rise to the appointment of a guardian *ad litem* and/or to separate legal representation of each party as described fully in the Magistrates' Court (Children and Young Persons) Rules 1988 para 16.

The procedure at the hearing is in two parts. First, the applicant should be called to give evidence to prove one of the primary grounds of the application. The child or his parents or their representatives may cross examine any of the witnesses called in the usual way, and members of the bench may put additional questions.

If a *prima facie* case has been made out then the respondents may call witnesses and give evidence or make a statement themselves. Whether or not any evidence is called the child or his representative may then address the court. A parent or guardian may at any time cross examine any witness as to any allegation made against him in the course of the proceedings, and may also make representations to the court at any stage after the conclusion of the evidence as the court considers appropriate.

After the evidence either party may with leave make a second address to the court, such leave also being granted to the other party. Where a guardian *ad litem* has been appointed, he will be given an opportunity to give any evidence relevant to the application which he is able to give at the conclusion of the evidence of the applicant and the respondent(s), but before any representations are made to the court.

Throughout the proceedings, the court has a duty to explain the nature of the proceedings to the child in terms suitable to his age and understanding. The child or parent may, however, be excluded from the court if the court considers it appropriate but have no power to see the child privately.

If the court finds the case proved it must then consider any reports available before deciding what order to make and, if necessary, the case can be adjourned for further reports. Before finally disposing of the case, the court must in simple language inform the child, his representative and his parent or guardian of their intention. They may then make representations before the order is finally given.

16 Magistrates' courts in England and Wales

England

Avon

Bath and North East Somerton Division

Bath
Tel: 01225 463281

Bristol Division

Bristol
Tel: 0117 943 5100

North Avon Division

Yate
Tel: 01454 310505

Woodspring Division

Weston-super-Mare
Tel: 01934 621 503

Bedfordshire

Bedford Division

Bedford
Tel: 01234 359422

Luton Division

Luton
Tel: 01582 24852

Berkshire

Forest Division

Bracknell
Tel: 01344 425051

Maidenhead Division

Maidenhead
Tel: 01628 30615

Reading Division

Reading
Tel: 01734 552600

Slough and Windsor Division

Slough
Tel: 01753 521345

West Berkshire Division

Newbury
Tel: 01635 43891

Buckinghamshire

Central Buckinghamshire Division

Aylesbury
Tel: 01296 82371

Milton Keynes Division

Milton Keynes
Tel: 01908 684901

Wycombe and Beaconsfield Division

High Wycombe
Tel: 01494 436335

Cambridgeshire

Cambridge Division

Cambridge
Tel: 01223 314311

Huntingdonshire Division

Huntingdon
Tel: 01480 451118

Peterborough Division

Peterborough
Tel: 01733 63971

Cheshire

Chester Division

Chester
Tel: 01244 310088

South Cheshire Division (Crewe and Congleton Divisions combined)

Crewe
Tel: 01270 256221

Halton Division

Runcorn
Tel: 01928 716130

Macclesfield Division

Macclesfield
Tel: 01625 610123

Vale Royal Division

Northwich
Tel: 01606 42809

Warrington Division

Warrington
Tel: 01925 653136

Cleveland

Hartlepool Division

Hartlepool
Tel: 01429 271451

Langbaugh East Division

Guisborough
Tel: 01287 632014

Teesside Division

Middlesborough
Tel: 01642 240301

Cornwall

East Penwith Division

Truro
Tel: 01872 74075

Falmouth and Kerrier Division (Falmouth-Penryn and Helston and Kerrier Divisions combined, Falmouth-Penryn Division is Falmouth and Penryn Divisions combined)

Truro
Tel: 01872 74075

Isles of Scilly Division

Truro
Tel: 01872 74075

Penwith Division

Truro
Tel: 01872 74075

Truro and South Powder Division (South Powder and Truro and West Powder Divisions combined)

Truro
Tel: 01872 74075

Cumbria

Appleby Division

Kendal
Tel: 01539 720478

Carlisle Division

Carlisle
Tel: 01228 27534

Furness and District Division

Barrow-in-Furness
Tel: 01229 820161

Kendal and Lonsdale Division

Kendal
Tel: 01539 720478

Keswick Division

Workington
Tel: 01900 62244

Penrith and Alston Division

Kendal
Tel: 01539 720478

South Lakes Division

Kendal
Tel: 01539 720478

West Allerdale Division

Workington
Tel: 01900 62244

Whitehaven Division

Workington
Tel: 01900 62244

Wigton Division

Carlisle
Tel: 01228 27534

Derbyshire

Chesterfield Division

Chesterfield
Tel: 01246 278171

Derby and South Derbyshire Division

Derby
Tel: 01332 292100

East Derbyshire Division

Ilkeston
Tel: 0115 932 0286

Glossop Division

Buxton
Tel: 01298 23951

High Peak Division

Buxton
Tel: 01298 23951

West Derbyshire Division

Buxton
Tel: 01298 23951

Devon

Barnstaple and South Molton Division(Barnstable and South Molton Divisions combined)

Barnstable
Tel: 01271 388461

Exeter and Wonford Division (Exeter and Wonford Divisions combined)

Exeter
Tel: 01392 70081

Plymouth Division

Plymouth
Tel: 01752 206200

Torbay Division

Torquay
Tel: 01803 298683

Dorset

Bournemouth and Christchurch Division

Bournemouth
Tel: 01202 745309

Central Dorset Division

Poole
Tel: 01202 745309

Poole Division

Poole
Tel: 01202 745309

West Dorset Division

Weymouth
Tel: 01305 783891

Weymouth and Portland Division

Weymouth
Tel: 01305 783891

Durham

Chester-le-Street Division

Chester-le-Street
Tel: 0191 388 4251/2

Darlington Division

Darlington
Tel: 01325 461231

Derwentside Division

Consett
Tel: 01207 502651

Durham Division

Durham
Tel: 0191 386 5178/9

Easington Division

Peterlee
Tel: 0191 518 2297

Sedgefield Division

Newton Aycliffe
Tel: 01325 318114

Teesdale and Wear Valley Division

Bishop Auckland
Tel: 01388 602488

East Sussex

Brighton and Hove Division

Brighton
Tel: 01273 670888

Eastbourne and Hailsham Division

Eastbourne
Tel: 01323 727518

Hastings and Rother Division

Hastings
Tel: 01424 437644

Lewes and Crowborough Division

Lewes
Tel: 01273 47889

Essex

Basildon Division

Basildon
Tel: 01268 293129

Colchester Division

Colchester
Tel: 01206 563057

Harlow Division

Harlow
Tel: 01279 425108

Rochford and Southend-on-Sea Division

Southend-on-Sea
Tel: 01702 348491

Gloucestershire

Forest of Dean Division (Coleford, Lydney and Newnham Divisions combined)

Coleford
Tel: 01594 32261

Gloucester Division

Gloucester
Tel: 01452 426130

North Gloucestershire Division

Cheltenham
Tel: 01242 532323

South Gloucestershire Division (Berkeley and Dursley, Whitminster and Stroud Divisions combined)

Stroud
Tel: 01453 765613

Greater Manchester

Bolton MD

Bolton
Tel: 01204 522244

Bury MD

Bury
Tel: 0161 764 3358

Manchester MD

Manchester
Tel: 0161 832 7272

Oldham MD

Oldham
Tel: 0161 620 2331

Rochdale MD

Rochdale
Tel: 01706 352442

Salford MD

Salford
Tel: 0161 834 9457

Stockport MD

Stockport
Tel: 0161 477 2020

Tameside MD

Bury
Tel: 0161 330 2023

Trafford MD

Sale
Tel: 0161 976 3333

Wigan Division

Wigan
Tel: 01942 243706

Hampshire

New Forest Division

Aldershot
Tel: 01252 366000

North West Hampshire Division

Basingstoke
Tel: 01252 366000

South East Hampshire Division

Portsmouth
Tel: 01705 819421

South Hampshire Division

Portsmouth
Tel: 01705 819421

Southampton Division

Southampton
Tel: 01703 635911

Hereford and Worcester

Bromsgrove and Redditch Division

Redditch
Tel: 01527 591035

Herefordshire Division

Hereford
Tel: 01432 276058

Severnminister Division

Redditch
Tel: 01527 591035

South Worcestershire Division

Droitwich
Tel: 01905 771089

Hertfordshire

Bishop's Stortford Division

Stevenage
Tel: 01438 730412

Cheshunt Division

Stevenage
Tel: 01438 730412

Dacorum Division

Watford
Tel: 01923 238111

North Hertfordshire Division

Stevenage
Tel: 01438 730412

St Albans and Mid Hertfordshire Division

St Albans
Tel: 01727 816822

Watford Division

Watford
Tel: 01923 238111

Humberside

Bainton, Wilton and Holme Beacon Division

Beverley
Tel: 01482 861607

Beverley Division

Beverley
Tel: 01482 861607

Dickering and Northern Holderness Division

Beverley
Tel: 01482 861607

Epworth and Goole Division

Scunthorpe
Tel: 01724 281100

Grimsby and Cleethorpes Division

Grimsby
Tel: 01472 358681

Kingston upon Hull Division

Kingston upon Hull
Tel: 01482 328914

Scunthorpe, Brigg and Barton Division

Scunthorpe
Tel: 01724 281100

South and Middle Holderness Division

Kingston upon Hull
Tel: 01482 328914

South Hunsley Beacon and Howdenshire Division

Beverley
Tel: 01482 861607

Isle of Wight

Isle of Wight Division

Newport
Tel: 01983 524244

Kent

Ashford and Tenterden Division

Folkestone
Tel: 01303 851371

Canterbury and St Augustine Division

Canterbury
Tel: 01227 454731

Dartford Division

Chatham
Tel: 01634 830232

Dover and East Kent Division

Folkestone
Tel: 01303 851371

Faversham and Sittingbourne Division

Sittingbourne
Tel: 01795 472138

Folkestone and Hythe Division

Folkestone
Tel: 01303 851371

Gravesham Division

Chatham
Tel: 01634 830232

Maidstone Division

Maidstone
Tel: 01622 671041

Medway Division

Chatham
Tel: 01634 830232

Sevenoaks Division

Maidstone
Tel: 01622 671041

Thanet Division

Margate
Tel: 01843 291775

Tonbridge and Malling Division

Maidstone
Tel: 01622 671041

Tunbridge Wells and Cranbrook Division

Maidstone
Tel: 01622 671041

Lancashire

Blackburn, Darwen and Ribble Valley Division

Blackburn
Tel: 01254 672216

Blackpool Division

Blackpool
Tel: 01253 757000

Burnley and Pendle Division

Burnley
Tel: 01282 610000

Chorley Division

Chorley
Tel: 01257 225000

Fylde Division

Fleetwood
Tel: 01253 875123

Lancaster Division

Lancaster
Tel: 01524 597000

Ormskirk Division

Ormskirk
Tel: 01695 572407

Preston Division

Preston
Tel: 01772 208000

Leicestershire

Ashby-de-la-Zouch Division

Coalville
Tel: 01530 810661

Leicester Division

Leicester
Tel: 0116 255 3666

Loughborough Division

Loughborough
Tel: 01509 215715

Lincolnshire

Boston Division

Boston
Tel: 01205 362852

Gainsborough Division

Gainsborough
Tel: 01427 615162

Grantham Division

Grantham
Tel: 01476 63438

Lincoln District Division

Lincoln
Tel: 01522 528218

Spilsby and Skegness Division

Skegness
Tel: 01754 762692

Inner London

South Westminster Division
Bow Street Magistrates' Court

Bow Street WC2E
Tel: 0171 379 4713

Horseferry Road Magistrates' Court

Horseferry Road SW1P
Tel: 0171 233 2000

North Westminster Division
Marylebone Magistrates' Court

Marylebone Road NW1
Tel: 0171 706 1261

West London Division
West London Magistrates' Court

Southcombe Street W14
Tel: 0171 371 1222

West Central Division
Clerkenwell Magistrates' Court

Kings Cross Road WC1X
Tel: 0171 278 6541

Hampstead Magistrates' Court

Hampstead NW3
Tel: 0171 435 1436

East Central Division
Highbury Corner Magistrates' Court

Holloway Road N7
Tel: 0171 607 6757

Thames Division
Thames Magistrates' Court

Bow Road E3
Tel: 0181 980 1000

South Western Division
South Western Magistrates' Court

Lavender Hill SW11
Tel: 0171 228 9201

South Central Division
Camberwell Green Magistrates' Court

Camberwell Green SE5
Tel: 0171 703 0909

Tower Bridge Magistrates' Court

Tooley Street SE1
Tel: 0171 407 4232

South Eastern Division
Greenwich Magistrates' Court

Greenwich SE10
Tel: 0181 694 0033

Woolwich Magistrates' Court

Woolwich SE18
Tel: 0181 855 8518

Outer London

Barking and Dagenham PSA

Barking
Tel: 0181 594 5311

Hendon MC

Hendon
Tel: 0181 441 9042

Bexley PSA

Bexleyheath
Tel: 0181 304 5211

Brent PSA

Church End NW10
Tel: 0181 451 7111

Bromley PSA

Bromley
Tel: 0181 325 4000

Croydon PSA

Croydon
Tel: 0181 686 8680

Ealing PSA

Ealing
Tel: 0181 579 9311

Enfield MC

Tottenham
Tel: 0181 808 5411

Haringey MC

Highgate
Tel: 0181 340 3472

Harrow MC

Harrow
Tel: 0181 427 5146

Havering MC

Romford
Tel: 01708 771771

Hillingdon PSA

Uxbridge
Tel: 01895 230771

Hounslow PSA
Feltham MC

Feltham
Tel: 0181 890 4811

Brentford MC

Brentford
Tel: 0181 568 9811

Kingston-upon-Thames PSA

Kingston-upon-Thames
Tel: 0181 546 5603

Merton PSA

Wimbledon
Tel: 0181 946 8622

Newham PSA

Stratford
Tel: 0181 522 5000

Redbridge PSA

Ilford
Tel: 0181 551 4461

Richmond-upon-Thames PSA

Richmond
Tel: 0181 948 2101

Sutton PSA

Wallington
Tel: 0181 770 5950

Waltham Forest PSA

Walthamstow
Tel: 0181 527 8000

Merseyside

Knowsley MD

Huyton
Tel: 0151 489 4558

Liverpool MD

Liverpool
Tel: 0151 243 5500

St Helens MD

St Helens
Tel: 01744 20244

Sefton MD
South Sefton District

Bootle
Tel: 0151 933 6999

Wirral MD

Birkenhead
Tel: 0151 647 2345

Norfolk

Central Norfolk Division

Thetford
Tel: 01842 754941

Great Yarmouth Division

Great Yarmouth
Tel: 01493 851127

Norwich Division

Norwich
Tel: 01603 632421

South Norfolk Division

Thetford
Tel: 01842 754941

Northamptonshire

Northampton Division

Northampton
Tel: 01604 497000

Northumberland

Alnwick Division

Alnwick
Tel: 01665 602727

Berwick-upon-Tweed Division

Berwick-upon-Tweed
Tel: 01289 306885

South East Northumberland Division

Bedlington
Tel: 01670 531100

Tynedale Division

Hexham
Tel: 01434 603248/603659

North Yorkshire

Easingwold Division

Thirsk
Tel: 01845 522587

Northallerton Division (Stokesley, Allertonshire, Birdforth, Gilling East, Hallikeld and Hang East Divisions combined)

Thirsk
Tel: 01845 522587

Richmond Division

Thirsk
Tel: 01845 522587

Nottinghamshire

East Retford Division

Worksop
Tel: 01909 486111

Mansfield Division

Mansfield
Tel: 01623 451500

Nottingham Division

Nottingham
Tel: 0115 955 8111

Oxfordshire

Banbury Division

Banbury
Tel: 01295 256193

Bicester Division

Bicester
Tel: 01869 243181

Oxford Division

Oxford
Tel: 01865 815922/0

Abingdon, Didcot and Wantage Division (Abingdon and Didcot and Wantage Divisions combined, Didcot and Wantage Division is Moreton and Wallingford and Wantage and Faringdon Divisions combined, Wantage and Faringdon Division is a further combination of Faringdon and Wantage Divisions)

Wantage
Tel: 01235 765311

Witney Division

Witney
Tel: 01993 704488

Shropshire

Drayton Division

Shrewsbury
Tel: 01743 458500

Shrewsbury Division

Shrewsbury
Tel: 01743 458500

Telford Division

Telford
Tel: 01952 204500

Somerset

Taunton Deane Division

Taunton
Tel: 01823 257084

West Somerset Division

Taunton
Tel: 01823 257084

South Somerset Division (Ilminster, Somerton, Wincanton and Yeovil Divisions combined)

Yeovil
Tel: 01935 26281

South Yorkshire

Barnsley District

Barnsley
Tel: 01226 243151

Doncaster Division

Doncaster
Tel: 01302 340323

Rotherham Division

Rotherham
Tel: 01709 839339

Sheffield District

Sheffield
Tel: 0114 276 0760

Staffordshire

Burton-upon-Trent Division

Lichfield
Tel: 01543 264124

Cannock Division

South Walls
Tel: 01785 223144

Lichfield Division

Lichfield
Tel: 01543 264124

Newcastle-under-Lyme and Pirehill North Division

Newcastle-under-Lyme
Tel: 01782 628015

Rugeley Division

Lichfield
Tel: 01543 264124

Stoke-on-Trent Division

Stoke-on-Trent
Tel: 01538 382713

Tamworth Division

Lichfield
Tel: 01543 264124

Suffolk

Deben Division

Ipswich
Tel: 01473 217261

North East Suffolk Division

Lowestoft
Tel: 01502 501060

North West Suffolk Division

Bury St Edmunds
Tel: 01284 763141

Surrey

North and East Surrey Division

Staines
Tel: 01784 459261

North West Surrey Division

Woking
Tel: 01483 714950

South East Surrey Division

Redhill
Tel: 01737 765581

South West Surrey Division

Guildford
Tel: 01483 34811

Tyne and Wear

Gateshead MD

Gateshead
Tel: 0191 477 5821

Newcastle Upon Tyne MD

Newcastle Upon Tyne
Tel: 0191 232 7326/7

North Tyneside MD

North Shields
Tel: 0191 296 0099

South Tyneside MD

Hebburn
Tel: 0191 483 4321

Sunderland MD
Sunderland Division

Sunderland
Tel: 0191 514 1621

Warwickshire

Mid-Warwickshire Division

Leamington Spa
Tel: 01926 429133

Nuneaton Division

Nuneaton
Tel: 01203 382750

West Midlands

Birmingham MD
Birmingham Division

Birmingham
Tel: 0121 212 6600

Sutton Coldfield Division

Sutton Coldfield
Tel: 0121 354 7777

Coventry MD
Coventry District

Coventry
Tel: 01203 630666

Dudley MD
Dudley Division

Dudley
Tel: 01384 211411/2/3/4

Halesowen Division

Halesowen
Tel: 0121 550 1141

Stourbridge Division

Stourbridge
Tel: 01384 378282

Sandwell MD
Warley Division

Warley
Tel: 0121 511 2222

West Bromwich Division

West Bromwich
Tel: 0121 569 5827/8

Solihull MD
Solihull District

Solihull
Tel: 0121 705 8101

Walsall MD
Aldridge and Brownhills Division

Aldridge
Tel: 01922 54242

Walsall Division

Walsall
Tel: 01922 38222

Wolverhampton MD
Wolverhampton District

Wolverhampton
Tel: 01902 773151

West Sussex

Arundel and Chichester and District Division

Chicester
Tel: 01243 817000

Crawley Division

Crawley
Tel: 01293 895315

Horsham Division

Horsham
Tel: 01403 252391

Mid-Sussex Division

Haywards Heath
Tel: 01444 417611

Worthing and District Division

Worthing
Tel: 01903 210981

West Yorkshire

Bradford MD
Calderdale Division

Halifax
Tel: 01422 360695

Kirklees MD
Huddersfield Division

Huddersfield
Tel: 01484 423552/3/4

Leeds MD

Leeds
Tel: 0113 245 9653

Wakefield MD

Batley
Tel: 01924 424030

Wiltshire

North Wiltshire Division

Chippenham
Tel: 01249 654361

Salisbury Division

Salisbury
Tel: 01722 333225

Swindon Division

Swindon
Tel: 01793 527281/2

West Wiltshire Division

Trowbridge
Tel: 01225 713508/9

Wales

Clwyd

Colwyn Division

Denbigh
Tel: 01745 812651

Flint Division

Mold
Tel: 01352 752757

Mold Division

Mold
Tel: 01352 752757

Rhuddlan Division

Prestatyn
Tel: 01745 855931

Wrexham Maelor Division

Wrexham
Tel: 01978 291855

Dyfed

Carmarthen North Division

Carmarthen
Tel: 01267 222050

Carmarthen South Division

Carmarthen
Tel: 01267 222050

Ceredigion Ganol Division

Aberaeron
Tel: 01545 570886

Cleddau Division

Haverfordwest
Tel: 01437 766451

Dinefwr Division

Llanelli
Tel: 01554 757201

Gogledd Preseli Division

Haverfordwest
Tel: 01437 766451

South Pembrokeshire Division

Haverfordwest
Tel: 01437 766451

Gwent

Bedwellty Division

Tredegar
Tel: 01495 72201

East Gwent Division

Cwmbran
Tel: 01633 869431

Lower Rhymney Valley Division

Tredegar
Tel: 01495 72201

Newport Division

Newport
Tel: 01633 213361

Upper Rhymney Valley Division

Tredegar
Tel: 01495 72201

Gwynedd

Aberconwy Division

Llandudno
Tel: 01492 871333

Bangor Division

Caernarfon
Tel: 01286 675200

Caernarfon and Gwyrfai Division

Caernarfon
Tel: 01286 675200

Eifinydd and Pwllheli Division

Caernarfon
Tel: 01286 675200

Merionnydd Division

Llandudno
Tel: 01492 871333

Ynys Mòn/Anglesey Division

Llandudno
Tel: 01492 871333

Powys

Brecon Division

Brecon
Tel: 01874 622993

Newtown Division

Newtown
Tel: 01686 627150

Welshpool Division

Newtown
Tel: 01686 627150

South Wales

Cardiff Division

Cardiff
Tel: 01222 463040

Cynon Valley Division

Aberdare
Tel: 01685 883688

Merthyr Tydfil Division

Merthyr Tydfil
Tel: 01685 721731

Miskin Division

Cardiff
Tel: 01443 480750

Vale of Glamorgan Division

Barry
Tel: 01446 737491

West Glamorgan

Neath Port Talbot Division

Neath
Tel: 01639 637981

Swansea County Division

Swansea
Tel: 01792 655171

17 Further reading

Archbold, *Pleading, Evidence and Practice in Criminal Cases*, 43rd edn, Sweet & Maxwell, 1988

Bing, *Criminal Procedure and Sentencing in the Magistrates' Court*, 4th edn, Sweet & Maxwell, 1996

Davies and Mornington, *Matrimonial Proceedings*, 2nd edn, Longman, 1991

Halnan and Wallis, *Wilkinson's Road Traffic Offences*, 14th edn, Longman, 1989

Hannibal and Hardy, *Road Traffic Law*, 2nd edn, Cavendish, 1996

Mitchels, *Child Care and Protection, Law and Practice*, 2nd edn, Cavendish, 1996

Moiser and Philips, *Practice and Procedure in Magistrates' Courts,* 3rd edn, Fourmat, 1992

Moore, *Anthony and Berryman's Magistrates' Court Guide*, Butterworths, 1996.

Moore and Wilkinson, *Youth Court: A Guide to the Law and Practice*, 2nd edn, Longman, 1994

Richman and Draycott, *Stone's Justices' Manual 1988*, Butterworth